HIGHLAND RAILWAY MISCELLANY

A pictorial record of
the Company's
activities
in the public eye and
behind the scenes

Peter Tatlow

**Oxford Publishing
Company**

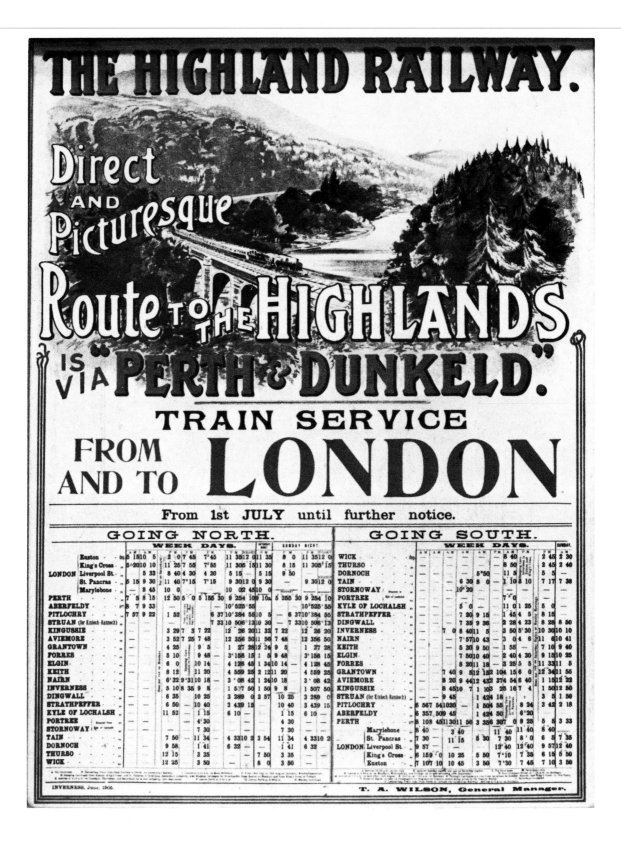

CONTENTS

		Plates
Preface		
The System		2–33
Motive power		34–82
Rolling stock		83–88
Civil Engineering:	Buildings	89–117
	Signal cabins	118–126
	Viaducts	127–141
	Bridges	142–156
	Permanent way	157–162
Lineside		163–180
Signalling		181–196
Operating		197–219
Hazards		220–232
Shipping activities		233–235
Hotels		236–241
Publicity		242–247
Railway Staff		248–251
Tickets		252–260
Luggage labels		261–271
Spotlight on . . .	Aviemore	272–273
	Blair Atholl	274–277
	Dingwall	278–279
	Inverness	280–285
	Killiecrankie	286–290
	The Skye Line	291–292
	The Mound	293–294
Acknowledgements		295

BYE-LAWS AND REGULATIONS

MADE BY THE

HIGHLAND RAILWAY COMPANY,

With the approval of the Board of Trade, for Regulating the Travelling upon and using of all Railways belonging to, or leased to, the said Company, and with respect to which that Company have power to make Bye-laws.

Given under the common seal of the Highland Railway Company the 23d day of October 1874.

AND. DOUGALL, Secretary of the Company.

The Board of Trade hereby signify their allowance and approval of the above Bye-laws and Regulations.
Signed by order of the Board of Trade this 31st day of October 1874.

HENRY G. CALCRAFT, an Assistant Secretary to the Board of Trade.

NOTICES.

PREFACE

In compiling this work on the Highland Railway in the Oxford Publishing Company's *Miscellany* series, I am conscious that it has been preceeded in the field by works devoted to the larger railway companies of the British Isles. These prior works have often been produced in two volumes, plus in most cases individual works on coaches, wagons, signalling, architecture, road vehicles, station layouts, etc. Compared to the Great Western, LNWR, LMS and L & Y, already covered in this series, the Highland Railway was a small concern and, although popular, hardly merits separate books devoted solely to these subjects.

OPC have already shown their confidence in the Highland Railway by publishing my revision of M.V.C. Allchin's 'A History of Highland Locomotives' in 1979 and initially it was my intention that all the remaining aspects, including a selection of drawings, should be dealt with in one volume under the heading of *Miscellany*. However, as material accumulated it became apparent that Highland rolling stock would have to be the subject of a separate work and it is planned that in due course details of HR coaches and wagons will be properly presented and illustrated. Likewise, it has been found that the proposed selection of track diagrams, station layouts and drawings of various static items of equipment and buildings must await a pictorial line survey.

The first constituent of the Highland Railway to be built – the Inverness and Nairn Railway – opened its doors to business on November 6, 1855 at a time when photography was still in its infancy. Whilst, before the turn of the century, professional photographers were established throughout the land (together with a few talented amateurs) their work tended to portray the more official view of railways. It was not until the early decades of this century that photography generally became available to the public and those interested directed their cameras at the more everyday but nonetheless necessary, aspects of the railway scene. Therefore, although this book is concerned with all those things that made up the Highland Railway, many subjects were photographed after that company ceased to exist.

It is my contention that the spirit of the Highland Railway lived on after grouping in 1923 and was only slowly diluted by the London, Midland and Scottish Railway Company, in which it had been amalgamated. Of course the LMS quickly scrapped some ancient locomotives, coaches and wagons and the substantial numbers that survived were repainted in LMS liveries. There were some developments, such as the greater use of corridor trains and an increase in dining car facilities, together with the introduction of schemes to make greater use of equipment, which were for the good of travellers. However, much of the fixed equipment, lineside features, buildings and track layout remained largely unaltered. Likewise traffic patterns were generally similar, if a little reduced.

World War II did admittedly result in some alterations and additions to meet the exigencies of hostilities and changes were by then becoming noticeable in the motive power, rolling stock and signalling spheres; as life-expired equipment was renewed. However, it was really only with Beeching that much of the long familiar scene was swept away. It is perhaps only coincidence that at the same time the earlier replacement steam motive power was itself being displaced by the advent of the diesel era.

I find the early LMS period of what had by then become the Highland Section of the LMS Northern Division as fascinating as that of the Highland Railway itself and hope that readers will excuse the inclusion of a fair proportion of photographs taken after the Highland Railway had strictly speaking ceased to exist. In any case to the best of my knowledge to have relied solely on photographs taken before this period would have necessarily resulted in a somewhat slimmer book.

I trust that the contents of this volume will be of interest and value to readers. For much of it we turn our attention away from the glamour of locomotives and trains, and direct it to the multitude of other activities necessary for the proper and efficient running of the Highland Railway. In so doing, if it enlightens and brings pleasure, I shall be satisfied.

Peter Tatlow

Typesetting by: Spire Print Services Ltd, Salisbury, Wilts.

Printed in Great Britain by:
Netherwood Dalton & Co. Ltd., Huddersfield, Yorks.

Published by:
Oxford Publishing Co.
Link House
West Street
POOLE, Dorset

The System

Perth was situated on the Caledonian Railway's main line from Glasgow and the south to Aberdeen and thereby formed the northern stretch of the West Coast route. Perth General station, as well as being the CR's junction for the line to Dundee, was also used by the North British and the Highland railways. The NB's lines from Fife joined the CR at Hilton Jcn just south of Moncrief Tunnel, thereby permitting the East Coast and Midland companies access to the Highlands. All HR trains for the north commenced their journeys at Perth and exercised running powers over the CR's line to the north for the 7¼ miles to Stanley. The station, except the platforms serving the Caley's line to Dundee, was managed by a joint committee.

Plate 2 shows two of David Jones' 4-4-0s having arrived at Perth with a southbound train in July 1895. The leading engine is No. 89 *Sir George* of the 'Strath' class built by Neilson Reid and delivered in May 1892, whilst the second is No. 74 *Beaufort* of the 'Lochgorm Bogie' class so titled because they were built, over a number of years, at the Company's Lochgorm Works at Inverness, in this case being taken into traffic in September 1885. Both are in Jones' livery of apple green with broad olive green bands with thinner black edge bands, which were in turn picked out with white and vermillion lines. *Sir George* has tender rails, while *Beaufort* has yet to have them added. The latter engine was withdrawn in February 1915, whilst the younger survived into LMS days and carried No. 14271 until its demise in August 1930.

Plate 3: No. 67 *Cromartie* illustrates David Jones' first design of 4-4-0, the 'Duke' class supplied by Dübs in 1874. Indeed until January 1877 No. 67 carried the name *The Duke*. It is pictured in the 1890s standing in front of the recently completed Glasgow Road Bridge signal box waiting to take over a northbound train. Behind the signal box is the NB's goods yard and the presence of several cattle vans and a number of open wagons temporarily fitted out with rails for the conveyance of sheep, suggests one of the annual sheep sales of late spring or early autumn.

Plate 4 (*above*): In early LMS days No. 14392 *Loch Naver* in crimson lake livery is seen heading north with a local passenger train. As part of the LMS Northern Division's boiler standardisation scheme, the locomotive was rebuilt with a Caledonian boiler design originally intended for their $18\frac{1}{2} \times 26$ in goods class. Perth was an open station and the ticket platform adjacent to the Up Line can be seen to the left of the engine. The coach behind the platform is a Highland six wheeled third class saloon built in the late 1890s, whilst the leading coach of the train is an ex Lancashire and Yorkshire Railway 52 foot bogie brake composite to diagram 37 built in 1898.

Plate 5: Taken on July 22, 1932 from approximately the same spot as the previous photograph depicts a somewhat grimy No. 14767 *Clan Mackinnon* bringing an Up express past Dovecotland Jcn signal box, which controlled the entry to the former HR engine shed at Perth. The first coach in the train is a CR 12 wheeler, followed by two LNWR coaches.

Plate 6 illustrates a north-bound express train in late Highland days leaving the outskirts of Perth, headed by No. 127 *Loch Garry* followed by an unidentified 4-6-0 of the 'Castle II' class. The leading two corridor coaches are of Highland origin with two Caley next. Towards the rear of the train is a Pullman car providing refreshments. Note the oval shaped 'Engine following' board over the right hand buffer of the leading engine. See *Plate 197* for further details.

A little further along the Caley's double track main line David Jones' 1894 design of 4-6-0 'Big Goods' No. 106 is seen in **Plate 7** with a train of what appear to be either sheeted open fish trucks or vans for perishable goods. As such they were likely to be at least piped, if not fitted with automatic vacuum brake and possibly Westinghouse air brake as well. Engine lamp codes were not introduced until after grouping, when additional lamp irons were fitted. Although still in HR livery, No. 106 nonetheless carries its lamps in position for a fitted freight, fish or cattle train with continuous brake in not less than one third of the vehicles. Note that the engine also has brackets and fixing lugs on the sides of the smokebox to enable it to be equipped with a large snow plough.

The Highland Railway's route actually began at Stanley by diverging from the CR's main line through Strathmore towards Aberdeen. In **Plate 8** the contemporary passenger engine to the 'Big Goods', the 4-4-0 'Loch' class of 1896 – in the form of No. 127 *Loch Garry* – crosses on to the main line from the Up Loop with a mixed goods train, its starting signal being behind the overbridge. The placing of lamps on the left hand side of the cab roof and opposite side of the tender is Highland practice.

The layout at Stanley was unusual and as viewed in **Plate 9** (*below*), the Highland Up Loop is the furthest on the left with the Down Loop on the near side of the platform. The Caley's running lines are in the middle of the picture. As the upper quadrant signal arms indicate, the photograph was taken in November 1946. The station was closed on June 11, 1956.

From Stanley Jcn the Highland Railway's route, now on its own metals, turns towards Dunkeld – the gateway to the Grampian Mountains. The line passes along Strath Tay and **Plate 10** illustrates the small wayside station of Dalguise on this stretch of the line. The compact but comprehensive goods yard should be noted. The double height loading bank was necessary to enable sheep to be loaded into the double deck sheep trucks favoured by the economically minded HR.

Later the line follows the tributaries of the Tay, the rivers Tummel and Garry, as it heads into the mountains. **Plate 11** depicts the single track which threads the Pass of Killiecrankie beneath Ben Vrackie, from one of several Queen's views. From the viaduct the line passes through one of only three short tunnels on the system and enters Killiecrankie station.

PASS OF KILLIECRANKIE (QUEENS VIEW)

Three miles further down the line a 4-6-0 No. 14690 *Dalcross Castle* of the 'Castle II' class, built in 1913 and wearing the LMS crimson lake livery, is seen in **Plate 12** just east of Blair Atholl station, having crossed the River Tilt bridge with an Up through train. The leading coach is a Midland Clayton design clerestory corridor brake composite with square panels, followed by an ex North British corridor brake composite. The ornate castellated arches over each abutment of the bridge are an indication that the line is passing through the estate of the Duke of Atholl, whose seat was at Blair Castle.

As traffic increased, the original single track line reached its limiting capacity and the HR embarked upon the work of doubling various lengths of the line. In **Plate 13** two Scotch derricks, one steam driven, can be seen in the late 1890s handling the stone blocks arising from the widening of the line on Struan Bank, while a double headed train struggles up the Hill.

The line reached its summit in the Pass of Drumochter (or *Druimuachdar* for those who prefer the Gaelic spelling) at the watershed of the rivers Garry and Truim, between the mountains of the Boar of Badenoch and A'Bhuidheanach Bheag. In **Plate 14** (*above*) No. 149 *Duncraig Castle* stands at a signal, early this century with a train entirely composed of Highland stock. The first coach is the 6 wheeled first class saloon No. 56.

By January 1923, when **Plate 15** was taken, a notice board, advising passengers that they were passing the summit, had been erected. At an altitude of 1,484 feet above sea level, the summit was, and still is, the highest main line in the British Isles. This height was only exceeded in standard gauge by the CR's Wanlockhead and Leadhills Light Railway with an elevation of 1,498 feet, but this branch closed on the last day of 1938. Note the snow fence at the lineside.

In **Plate 16** No. 57 *Clan Cameron*, the last of the 4-6-0 'Clan' class, and then about two years old, threads Drumochter Pass with a Down train in 1923. Behind the tender is a 6 wheeled Caley double ended horse box followed by three HR bogie coaches dating from David Jones' final years in office.

The building of the main line from Dunkeld to Forres was undertaken in the remarkably short period of two years. Authorisation was received on July 22, 1861 and the completed line was opened in three sections, starting with Dunkeld to Pitlochry on June 1, 1863, followed by Aviemore to Forres on August 3 and the closing section from Pitlochry to Aviemore on September 9, 1863. The route was surveyed, designed and construction supervised by the civil engineer Joseph Mitchell. **Plate 17** illustrates a cutting being excavated near Kingussie.

From November 1, 1898 through trains to Inverness were able to take the Direct Line from Aviemore via Carrbridge and a new summit of 1,315 feet above sea level at Slochd. **Plate 18** is a view looking northwards from a point near Carrbridge as a south-bound train headed by a pair of Stanier 'Black 5s' crosses the bridge over the River Dulnain.

The Highland Railway made up for its deficiency in tunnels by a number of spectacular viaducts, several of which were to be found on the Direct Line. **Plate 19** shows 'Big Goods' No. 17925 drifting down from Slochd across Findhorn Viaduct in July 1938 with a goods train largely consisting of wagons, many of them of the end door variety. The nine span lattice girder viaduct is further illustrated in *Plate 137*.

The hub of the Highland Railway's system and administrative centre was Inverness, situated at the head of the Moray Firth and the Great Glen, giving communication with the West Coast of Scotland via the Caledonian Canal. Here the Direct Line rejoined the original line, making its way along the coast from Forres and the eastern connection to Keith, and was the starting point for the line to the north. **Plate 20** pictures 4-4-0T 'Yankee Tank' No. 15014 in LMS crimson lake livery pottering about with a few wagons on June 27, 1927. In the foreground are a row of old locomotive tenders and a rake of loco coal wagons. The yard behind the main lines contains a wide range of wagons from various railways, some still in pregrouping livery. These have been analysed and the significance of the proportions of the different companies represented are discussed in detail in *Model Railways* magazine March 1975 issue.

The Inverness and Perth Junction Railway's line, as built in 1863, continued from Aviemore up the Strathspey to Granton-on-Spey. The first station beyond Aviemore, Boat of Garten, was the junction for the Great North of Scotland Railway's Strathspey branch from Craigellachie. **Plate 21** depicts Boat of Garten station from the south prior to alterations to the hotel and the rebuilding of the station buildings following a fire in January 1904.

The I & PJR line joined the earlier Inverness and Aberdeen Junction Railway approximately half way along its length with a triangular junction at Forres. In **Plate 22** the first part of the overnight train from Inverness to Euston and Kings Cross, (via Forres) is seen at Forres in the 1930s. The leading engine is No. 14391 *Loch Shin* in rebuilt form followed by an unidentified 'Castle III' class. The fireboxes of both engines have just been stoked for the climb to Dava Summit which had an elevation of 1,052 feet above sea level. The train contains sleeping cars of both LMS and LNER origin, including a WCJS clerestory 12 wheeler.

The last short branch line opened by the Highland Railway, apart from the two nominally independent branches to Dornoch and Lybster authorised and constructed under the Light Railways Act of 1896, was the 1½ mile line from Gollanfield Junction to Fort George on the Moray Firth. This commenced operation on July 1, 1899. **Plate 23** (*below*) illustrates David Jones' 2-4-0 No. 29 *Raigmore* (II) standing at Fort George station.

From Inverness the line to the 'Further North' first headed westwards along the shores of the Beauly Firth, Dingwall being reached in 1863. Thirty one years later a branch line was opened along the peninsular on the north side of the Firth, known as the Black Isle. **Plate 24** shows the terminal station for the line at Fortrose before World War I with a cruiser and several destroyers anchored off-shore. From left to right the station buildings, turntable, goods shed, water tower and railwaymen's cottages can be discerned. A description of the line appeared in *The Journal of the Historical Model Railway Society* Vol. 8 No. 4, October–December 1973.

Plate 25 pictures Dingwall Station looking south on July 13, 1933. Behind the footbridge, goods shed and engine shed is the Ferintosh Distillery, with warehouses, loading bank and siding. From August 19, 1870 Dingwall was the junction for the Skye line to Strome Ferry, and later for Kyle of Lochalsh after the extension of the line on November 2, 1897. It was also the starting point for the Strathpeffer branch train, which diverged from the Skye line at Fodderty Junction.

Further up the route to the North the line was taken westwards again, this time to skirt the Dornoch Firth. **Plate 26** (*below*) depicts the scene at Bonar Bridge station, with a north-bound train stopped at the platform, probably in 1925. The first coach is a former LNWR brake composite No. 9792 to diagram D216 in LMS livery. Ahead of this is a LNWR 50 foot full brake to diagram D377 still in pregrouping livery.

Bonar-Bridge Station, Ardgay.

Having regained the east coast at the Mound, via Lairg, the line turns westward for the last time to head inland beside the River Helmsdale and skirt the high ground, which runs right up to the coast at Ord Point. The countryside becomes less inhabited and desolate, until following Forsinard it leaves the adjoining road to cross 17 miles of treeless wilderness. In **Plate 27** No. 14687 *Brahan Castle* is about to depart from Forsinard Station with a south-bound train on July 18, 1931. The level crossing for the road can be seen in the foreground.

The north-eastern tip of the Scottish mainland is, however, cultivated and hence populated, and the railway which reached the area in 1874, divided at Georgemas Junction to terminate at Thurso and Wick. The former station is shown in **Plate 28**. A couple of rakes of open fish trucks are visible, together with a pair of coaches of David Jones' design. The overall roof to the station should be noted.

On July 1, 1903 a branch, constructed as a light railway, was opened from Wick to Lybster, nearly 14 miles down the coast. In **Plate 29** (*above*) 'Yankee Tank' No. 15013 in LMS crimson lake livery is seen arriving at Wick off the branch with a mixed train of an ex L & Y 6 wheel 33 foot long third class coaches to Diagram 8, still gas lit and in pre-grouping livery, four covered goods vans and an ex MR 6 wheel clerestory passenger brake van complete the formation. On the left a 'Castle I' class 4-6-0 is at the entrance to the engine shed.

Plate 30 depicts another view of No. 15013, now having had its smokebox door number plate removed, with a similar train at Lybster. The coach is a LNWR double-ended slip coach. Note the flat bottom rail to the track and the shoring to the timber engine shed on the right.

Plate 31 is a third view of a 'Yankee Tank', this time No. 14, one of the later batch delivered in 1893 by Dübs, with larger tanks. It is standing at the head of its train at Strathpeffer on September 1, 1894. The leading vehicle is a 4 wheeled passenger brake van of David Jones' design.

From 1870 to 1897 the terminus of the Skye line was at Strome Ferry on the south side of Loch Carron. The presence of the skew overbridge behind the overall roof of the station and the track skirting the shoreline in the distance indicate that **Plate 32** dates from after the extension of the line to Kyle of Lochalsh. Prior to this steamers would regularly sail four days a week to Portree, calling at Plockton, Broadford and Raasay. Twice a week there was also a service to Stornoway. Other occasional sailings were extended from Portree to Gairloch, Aultbea and Poolewe. In front of the signal cabin on the bottom left of the picture the turntable to the engine shed is partly visible.

The eventual terminus of the line was Kyle of Lochalsh, seen in **Plate 33** early this century. The line along the rocky coast from Strome Ferry passes through a deep rock cutting to emerge onto the pier projecting into Loch Alsh. The coastal steamers for Broadford, Raasay, Portree, Stornoway, Tarbert (Harris), Rodel, Lochmaddy and Oban could now call direct at the pier on their way through the Sound of Sleat. A ferry service operated direct to Kyleakin from a slipway beside the Lochalsh Hotel.

Motive power

The first engine delivered to a constituent of the Highland Railway was a 2-2-2 named *Raigmore* (I), supplied to the Inverness & Nairn Railway by Hawthorn of Leith in September 1855. However, the steep gradients on the expanding system and increases in traffic rendered such engines with single driving wheels inappropriate and the Highland's first Locomotive Superintendent, William Stroudley, rebuilt No. 1 *Raigmore* in 1869 as the 2-4-0 seen in **Plate 34** (*above*). The extra set of driving wheels was taken from another member of the same class and the existing boiler, cylinders and frame reused. Although generally successful, the frames proved to be inadequate and the engine was withdrawn in 1873. Note the ornate lining out, especially at the corners.

Goods engines on the other hand were of the 2-4-0 wheel arrangement from the outset. The two supplied for the Inverness and Ross-shire Railway at the time of the opening of the Northern Line to Dingwall were of the No. 14 class. **Plate 35** illustrates No. 49 at Perth in Jones livery. This engine was built by Hawthorn in 1862 as No. 14 and became No. 32 prior to becoming No. 49. At first named *Loch* followed by *Evanton* it was withdrawn in 1901.

Well stocked by recent deliveries to the constituents of the Highland, Stroudley was not called upon during his brief sojourn at Lochgorm to design large locomotives. However, the boilers released by rebuilding the 'Raigmore' (I) class enabled him to initiate a design of 0-6-0 tank engine and this in turn was the basis for his famous 'Terriers' for the LBSC. **Plate 36** shows the second of the class No. 57 *Lochgorm* at Inverness shed in plain Drummond livery prior to having a coal bunker fitted.

It fell to Stroudley's successor, David Jones, to fulfil the requirement for further tender locomotives. He first undertook this task in 1874 with ten 4-4-0 engines of the 'Duke' class built by Dübs. **Plate 37** (*above*) shows No. 62 *Huntingtower* in Drummond's earlier livery with full lining. Note the lamps on the smokebox and tender side, together with alarm bell and Westinghouse brake pump.

In 1890 a need arose for a replacement engine on the Strathpeffer branch and a redundant boiler off No. 13, an early 2-2-2, was used on a diminutive 0-4-4ST saddle tank. When in 1901 this boiler required renewal, the engine was rebuilt as a side tank and two years later sent to the Lybster branch. **Plate 38** depicts the engine, No. 53, at this time.

To replace a pair of the first 2-2-2s, David Jones built two 2-4-0s in 1877. **Plate 39** (*below*) illustrates No. 29 *Raigmore* (II) in Drummond's later plain livery. This engine was sold in July 1912.

The small wheeled derivative of David Jones' 4-4-0 designs was the 'Skye Bogie' class first introduced in 1882. **Plate 40**, however, depicts LMS No. 14284 built in 1898 after Peter Drummond had taken charge of locomotive affairs at Inverness. It therefore exhibits some of his features such as a plain chimney, in lieu of the louvred variety, and the absence of the compensating beam between the coupled wheels. The tender on the other hand is of the type provided for the 'Duke' class in 1874.

The final design of locomotive with the Crewe front end was the 'Strath' class introduced by David Jones in 1892. **Plate 41** illustrates No. 96 *Glentilt* in plain green livery.

Rather different were the class of five 4-4-0T 'Yankee Tanks' designed for Uruguay, but never delivered. After an initial loan of two, the remainder were completed by the builders Dübs and supplied to the Highland in 1893. **Plate 42** shows No. 54 at Fort Augustus.

No. 115, an example of David Jones' famous 'Big Goods' class, is depicted in **Plate 43**. This group of fifteen engines, built by Sharp Stewart of Glasgow in 1894, was the first of the 4-6-0 wheel arrangement to run in Great Britain. No. 115 is seen at Perth engine shed in plain green livery probably shortly before grouping.

In 1896 the 4-4-0 passenger counterpart of the above class was introduced by Jones with fifteen locomotives supplied by Dübs, to which three further examples were added in 1917. No. 14392 *Loch Naver* is depicted in **Plate 44** at Blair Atholl, after having been reboilered by the LMS in 1927. Note that the tool box at the rear of the tender has been removed and the tanks extended. The coal rails are also full length.

Plate 45 illustrates the first of Peter Drummond's engines, No. 1 *Ben y-Gloe* of the 'Small Ben' class, at Perth. The original lever reversing gear has been replaced by a steam operated reverser, a later pattern of number plate fitted to the cabside, and the tender extended in the same manner as *Loch Naver* (*see Plate 44*).

No. 14398 *Ben Alder* is illustrated in **Plate 46** at Inverness shed on May 17 1928. It had recently been repainted in the LMS's then new all black livery, lined in red, for passenger engines. It still has a Highland boiler, but the safety valves have been moved from the dome to firebox. At the time it was coupled to an 8 wheel tender of 3,200 gallon capacity.

Plate 47 shows a 'Barney Goods', LMS No. 17702, at Inverness in 1930, still fitted with a water tube firebox and Highland boiler. One of the 'Barney Goods' fitted with a water tube firebox was to last until 1934 and it did not receive a Caley boiler until two years later, only to have a Highland one restored in 1943. Note the packing behind the buffers, the additional guard irons and ring around the smokebox door. The cabside numerals appear to be of 10 in size, rather than the more usual 12 or 14 in varieties

The HR's first design of 4-6-0 passenger engine and a development of the 'Big Goods' was Peter Drummond's 'Castle' class introduced in 1900. **Plate 48** shows No. 143 *Gordon Castle* of the initial batch supplied by Dübs, in pristine condition and fully lined out standing at the entrance to Inverness shed.

In **Plate 49** *Cawdor Castle* is seen a few years later in F. G. Smith's livery with 9 in painted numbers high on the cabside and 5 in bright metal numerals on the smokebox door, but still with HIGHLAND RAILWAY on the tender side.

Following the withdrawal of most of the early 2-4-0s, made redundant by the introduction of Peter Drummond's 'Small Ben' and 'Barney' classes, three spare boilers and various parts recovered from scrapped locomotives were assembled into the 'Scrap Tank' class of 0-6-0 shunting tanks. **Plate 50** depicts No. 22 of this class.

For use on the numerous short and lightly trafficked branch lines, some laid to the Light Railway Act construction standards, Peter Drummond introduced a class of four 'Passenger Tanks' in 1905. **Plate 51** illustrates the first of these No. 25 *Strathpeffer*, on which branch it served at the time.

Drummond's last design for the HR was a class of 0-6-4T 'Banking Tanks' of substantial proportions first introduced in 1909. **Plate 52** (*below*) depicts Nos. 42 and 65 outside Blair Atholl shed awaiting their turn of duty to assist trains up the 'Hill' on September 11, 1925.

Frederick G. Smith's six 'River' class locomotives, initially barred by the Civil Engineer from the Highland system due to their high static weight, returned following tests and reassessment by the LMS of the capacity of certain bridges, (*see section on* Bridges). **Plate 53** shows the first of these engines in LMS crimson lake livery.

The last design of locomotive to be introduced on to the Highland Railway and intended to fulfill the role of the banished 'Rivers', was the 'Clan' class. **Plate 54** (*below*) illustrates the first of these No. 49 *Clan Campbell*, built by Hawthorn Leslie in 1919. A member of the second batch supplied in 1921 by the same firm was No. 55 *Clan Mackinnon*, which is seen in **Plate 55** (*at foot of page*) at Perth in immaculate condition.

The banishment of the 'River' class engines in 1915 came on top of an already critical situation in the Locomotive Department, due to a vast increase in traffic arising from the war effort and a serious backlog of repairs to the HR's existing locomotives. Through the auspices of the Railway Executive Committee, it was arranged for engines from other companies to be loaned to the Highland. Naturally these turned out to be not the most modern examples and **Plate 56** shows an unidentified LSWR 4-4-2T Adams 'Radial' and NER 0-4-4T Fletcher 'BTP' class No. 951 taking water at Blair Atholl on their way south in August 1921.

Following amalgamation in 1923, the LMS allocated some members of its early standard designs to various sections on the system. Thus the Highland Section acquired a few Fowler 4F 0-6-0 locomotives. An example, in **Plate 57**, is No. 4318 topping Druimuachdar Summit with a goods train in 1937.

A number of Fowler 3F 0-6-0Ts were also sent North and **Plate 58** depicts No. 7333 outside Lochgorm Works, Inverness on station pilot duties.

As older Highland engines were withdrawn, pre-grouping engines from other constituents of the LMS Northern Division were drafted in as replacements. Due to their numbers, the standardisation of their boilers and general ruggedness of construction, these usually turned out to be from the Caley. **Plate 59** (*above*) illustrates No. 17648 of McIntosh's '30' class 0-6-0 superheated goods built at St. Rollox in 1912 and photographed at Inverness in 1930.

No. 15103 in **Plate 60** was one of Dugald Drummond's diminutive '171' class of 0-4-4Ts built in 1886, seen taking water at Dingwall.

To work the Inverness Harbour branch a variety of four-coupled saddle tanks were sent from time to time and **Plate 61** (*below*) shows No. 16040 an ex-GSWR 0-4-0ST built by Andrews, Barr in 1881 and withdrawn in 1932. It is seen here shunting at Millburn in 1930.

For a time one of the pair of CR '262' class or 'Killin Tanks', No. 15001, was shedded at Inverness and **Plate 62** shows this engine there in June 1936. It was built at St. Rollox in 1885 and withdrawn in 1947.

Mechanically similar to the 'Killin Tanks', were the '264' class, which had been derived from an earlier Neilson standard design. Batches continued to be built by both Dugald Drummond and J. F. McIntosh until 1908 by which time a total of 34 had been constructed. In **Plate 63** No. 16011, also built in 1885, stands on the turntable at Inverness.

Three years after his move in 1912 from the Highland to the Glasgow and South Western Railway, Peter Drummond introduced a development of his last locomotive design for the HR, the 0-6-4T 'Banking Tank', in the form of a 0-6-2T, the '45' class. As well as the smaller wheel arrangement, the wheel base was 6 inches shorter; however the boilers were sufficiently similar to allow the latter to be fitted to the HR engines. As the Highland engines were withdrawn, the GSWR types, including examples of Whitelegg's amended design, were sent to Blair Atholl. **Plate 64** depicts No. 16913, built in 1917 and withdrawn in January 1938, with HR wooden snow ploughs in the left foreground.

From August 1934 the class of engines that was in due course to predominate in the Highlands, until the demise of steam in 1963, arrived in the form of Stanier's 4-6-0 5P5F, or as they were subsequently known 'Black 5'. **Plate 65** shows No. 5029 of this class built by Vulcan Foundary in 1934 and still in original condition departing from Blair Atholl with a train for the South.

Following the withdrawal of the last of the HR 'Passenger Tanks' early in 1957 with a broken crank axle, some Great Western Railway 0-6-0PT pannier tanks were sent North to operate the Dornoch branch. **Plate 66** shows No. 1649 standing outside the shed at Dingwall.

Various classes of Caley 4-coupled bogie engines, originally built for express duties, worked out their mileage on the Highland Section. **Plate 67** (*below*) illustrates a Pickersgill 4-4-0, No. 54487, waiting at the head of a ballast train at Dingwall to head down the Syke line on July 9, 1958. Built by Armstrong Whitworth in 1921, it was withdrawn in March 1961.

To service and maintain the Highland's stock of locomotives required the provision of numerous engine sheds throughout the system. One of the largest of these was at Perth to provide the bulk of motive power at the southern end of the main line. This depot, like the goods yard, was genuine HR owned property, albeit separated from the rest of the system by the 7 miles of CR line to Stanley. A broad selection of HR engines are captured in **Plate 68** (*above*) at Perth shed in 1908 or 1909. From left to right there are: an unidentified 'Castle', No. 144 *Blair Castle*, No. 66 *Ben Mholach*, No. 140 *Taymouth Castle*, No. 146 *Skibo Castle*, No. 119 *Loch Insh*, No. 104 and No. 126 *Loch Tummel*. All appear to be in Drummond's later plain livery.

About 50 years later, Aviemore, another of the HR's larger depots, is depicted in **Plate 69** with ex CR 0-6-0 class '812' No. 57586 and 4-6-0 'Black 5' No. 45465 on shed. This building now serves as the centre of locomotive affairs for the Strathspey Railway's preserved line to Boat of Garten.

As **Plate 70** shows, locomotive repairs and intermediate overhauls continued to be carried out in the Lochgorm Works at Inverness. On June 18, 1937 No. 14692 *Darnaway Castle* and a 'Superheated Goods' were receiving attention.

Plate 71 pictures the small stone built two road shed at Tain during the early LMS period with 'Small Ben' No. 14409 *Ben Alisky* resting between duties. The home signal for the line from the south is on the right.

At Dunrobin the Duke of Sutherland had a shed in which were kept his two saloon coaches. **Plate 72** illustrates this diminutive shed in 1954 after his privately owned locomotive *Dunrobin* and the 4 wheeled saloon had emigrated to New Romney. They were later to cross the Atlantic to find a new home in British Columbia, while the bogie saloon is at the National Railway Museum, York.

Probably little larger was the timber shed at Dornoch to house the branch line engine. **Plate 73** (*below*) shows 'Passenger Tank' No. 55051, the terminus station and goods shed on September 10, 1953. This area is now the site of a small industrial estate.

The three most northerly sheds in the British Isles are illustrated in **Plates 74 to 76**. Wick on the June 24, 1933, is shown in **Plate 74** (*above*) with two 4-6-0 'Castle' class locomotives being inspected by a party of enthusiasts. On the left are several tool vans and loco coal wagons.

Plate 75 (*left*) shows LMS Stanier 2-6-2T No. 40150 at Thurso in 1954, positioned approximately over the site of the former turntable. Finally, **Plate 76** (*below*) illustrates Lybster shed on July 18, 1931. This was a similar shed to Dornoch, but with the addition of some wind bracing. The locomotive is 'Passenger Tank' No. 15053 which is standing in front of the water tower.

Plate 77 shows work in progress on the installation of the new 63ft 4in diameter turntable at the centre of the well known Inverness round house on April 27, 1914. The Highland's 15 ton Cowans, Sheldon steam breakdown crane, seen standing on cribwork formed of old sleepers, is ready to position the centre pin for the new table, which was also supplied by Cowans, Sheldon. Construction of the masonry perimeter walls to the enlarged pit is also in hand, for which purpose Scotch derricks have been temporarily erected.

Manual coaling of locomotives continued at Inverness until the mid '30s, when the LMS constructed a mechanical coaling plant. Plate 78 depicts the old coaling stage in 1931, with the tender of No. 14395 *Loch Garve* being replenished from the series of tubs which were filled from the raised line of loco coal wagons at the rear of the stage. This locomotive was one of the 1917 batch supplied by the North British Loco Company and equipped with Westinghouse brake and enlarged tenders.

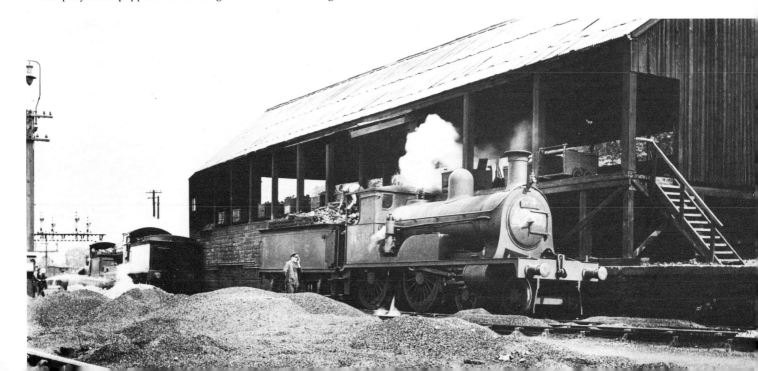

The need to refill locomotive's water tanks at intermediate points along the lines led to the installation of water tanks and columns at various points, usually stations. The Highland had a distinctive design of cast iron water column, which encompassed a stove to be used during cold weather to prevent the stand pipe freezing up. **Plate 79** (*above left*) illustrates the classical column style. This example was photographed at Georgemas Junction in August 1960. Another design of cap is seen in **Plate 80** (*above right*) which shows a column at Dunkeld with a domed shaped cap and knob. Whereas the previous and subsequent columns had lever operated water valves, this one has a turn cock on a short standard mounted on an extension to the base plate. Finally, **Plate 81** (*below left*) illustrates the commonest variety of water column, the round capped type, seen here at Dalguise. The 'A' numbers were for a reference scheme set up by the LMS. All columns had to be fed from a water tank and occasionally the tank was positioned adjacent to the track, thereby permitting the canvas bag to be fitted direct, as in **Plate 82** (*below right*) at Garve in July 1958.

Rolling stock

One of Peter Drummond's lavatory composite bogie coaches is illustrated in **Plate 83**. Formerly No. 77, built by R. Y. Pickering of Wishaw in 1904, the lower panelling has been replaced by match boarding. At first renumbered 18684 by the LMS, it is seen here with its second LMS number 19986. Fitted with dual brakes, steam heating and electric lighting in lieu of the original gas, it is still in the LMS livery style with full lining. This coach was withdrawn in August 1949.

Ten years later R. Y. Pickering supplied the corridor composite depicted in **Plate 84**. Originally No. 81, it was renumbered by the LMS firstly No. 18688 and in 1933 became No. 4996. The third compartment from the right had been downrated from first class when photographed in 1948. Withdrawal of the vehicle occurred in October 1952. Note the distinctive steam pipe below the solebar.

The last HR passenger rated stock in revenue earning service were three travelling post office vans built by the Company at its Needlefield Works in 1916. **Plate 85** shows No. M30323, formerly HR No. 10 and LMS (1st series) No. 7363, leaving Inverness for Perth on the afternoon of July 21, 1958. All three vans were replaced by BR vehicles and subsequently withdrawn in December 1961. They were originally equipped with mail pick-up apparatus at the right hand end, whilst the left as well as the right hand door also had a pair of traductor arms. Lineside apparatus was provided at Dunkeld, Pitlochry, Ballinluig, Dalwhinnie, Newtonmore and Kincraig on the Downside in all cases.

A number of 8 ton, 15ft 6in long, 2 plank ballast wagons with falling sides and ends survived in the service of the Engineer's Department for many years. **Plate 86** shows No. D297205 in the early '50s. Note the plate over the left hand axle box to prevent ballast particles entering the journal.

Although not the exclusive type used, the Highland is best known for its 6 wheeled goods brake van with a birdcage roof lookout. **Plate 87** is of the shorter, 20 foot long, 20 ton type. In this case it is the later version with a steel underframe and wings to the lookout to enable the guard to mount his perch without knocking his head. Many earlier vans were also altered to this arrangement. No. M-D294038 became a tool van at Aviemore and as such lasted until the early '50s. Passengers were permitted to travel in brake vans of goods trains, when there was no convenient passenger train, provided they accepted all risks and paid a first class fare.

Several coal merchants based on the Highland system possessed a limited number of private owner wagons. **Plate 88** depicts No. 3, a 10 ton, 5 plank, mineral wagon built by Hurst Nelson of Motherwell for John Smith & Sons coal, lime and potato merchants of Aberfeldy. It has a shallow curve to the ends of the bodywork and lever brakes acting on two wheels, but on one side only.

CIVIL ENGINEERING –
Buildings

Ballinluig was the junction for the 8¾ mile long branch to Aberfeldy opened on July 3, 1865 and closed just short of a century later on May 3, 1965. **Plate 89** shows the downside station buildings at Ballinluig on May 23, 1955 with the branch line behind. Note the Highland style platform seats, barrows and bracket lamps. The platform walls are, on the other hand, of recent construction.

At the outset the branch had only one intermediate station, at Grandtully, but on December 2, 1935 the LMS opened a halt at Balnaguard between Ballingluig and Grandtully. **Plate 90** illustrates the timber platform and simple facilities as they were on May 28, 1960.

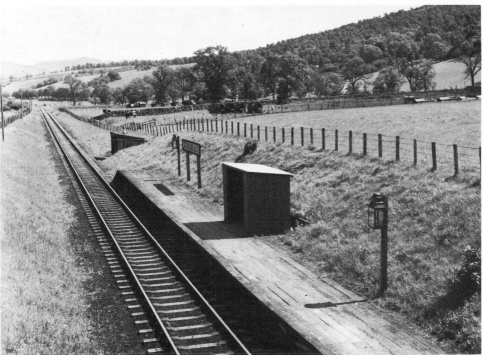

The line terminated at Aberfeldy with the single face platform and stone built station buildings depicted in **Plate 91**. These were reconstructed following a fire in 1929. As well as the usual goods facilities, there was an engine shed for the overnight stabling of the branch line engine, whilst half a mile back down the branch a private siding served a distillery owned by Dewars.

A unique station building on the line was Blair Atholl, which with the intention of pleasing the Duke of Atholl, was finished in the Swiss style. In **Plate 92** the station staff can be seen in casual stance on the platform in Highland days. Although the building still stands, economies in maintenance have led to the removal of the decorated bargeboards and the trimming back of the oversailing roof, resulting in a hideous elevation. Note the low height of the platform, which was typical of the Highland. Many remained unraised until BR days.

At an altitude of 1,405 feet above sea level Dalnaspidal was, from its opening on July 3, 1865 until its closure on May 3, 1965, the highest main line station in the British Isles. **Plate 93** shows from left to right the footbridge, railwaymen's cottages and the Post Office on the platform. During the winter of 1976/77 the station buildings were dismantled and removed to Aviemore for subsequent erection as the Strathspey Railway's station premises. The platform in this instance is also fairly low and constructed of old sleepers.

The station buildings at Newtonmore were rebuilt in 1893 and **Plate 94** illustrates them on July 11, 1957. The BR enamel name boards, mounted below the clock and elsewhere, have white letters and border on a light blue ground for the Scottish Region. The initials of the original owners are carved in the dark grey stonework on the gable end. Note the hurley type wheel barrow and the drinking fountain behind it.

Of similar vintage, but of timber construction, were the enlarged station facilities at Aviemore. These were constructed when Aviemore became the junction at the southern end of the Direct Line, initially in July 1892 with the opening of the line as far as Carrbridge. Once the new line to Inverness was opened in its entirety (on November 1, 1898) trains via the alternative routes were remarshalled here. **Plate 95** is a view looking south as the reconstruction is nearing completion. However the platform has yet to be surfaced and the finishing coats of paint applied.

A new station on the Direct Line was Dava. Seen in **Plate 96** on June 18, 1937, the footbridge – from the entrance and main buildings – leads to a simple timber waiting room. Behind is a cast iron water tank on a stone tower. The starting signal is positioned on the off side of the track to aid sighting round the curve.

On this page are two views of the station square at Inverness. The first, **Plate 97**, was photographed in 1863 presumably in connection with the opening of the through line to Perth. It shows the scene with single storey buildings, including A. W. Fraser's photographic studio, and a wall on the site of the company's future offices.

Plate 98 depicts the same location more than 40 years later after the building of the company's office on the left, the erection of the Cameron Statue in 1893 and the railway owned Station Hotel, the entrance to which is on the right. Three horse drawn cabs await a fare and the usual collection of bystanders exchange gossip.

Station Square, Inverness.

Several station buildings of an 'H' shape in plan have already been illustrated. **Plate 99** is of another, at Elgin, with a colonnade between the wings to provide some shelter for passengers and their luggage. Elgin was a point of interchange with the GNSR's Coast and Craigellachie Lines. Their station was off to the right.

When the line from Inverness to Nairn was extended to Elgin in 1858, it was proposed that the line to Perth should diverge at Nairn. However, by the time construction came to be undertaken in 1861, the authorised junction was altered to Forres. A deviation and new station were therefore put in hand to provide connection eastwards and westwards, leaving the old station isolated as seen in **Plate 100**. Certain features of its design, such as the colonnade, window mouldings and triple flue chimney stacks, are common with Elgin even if the plan layout is different.

Again following the 'H' plan were the station buildings at Nairn, shown in **Plate 101** during early BR days. The gable ends, colonnade and chimneys, however, are in a totally different style. The railwayman on the bicycle is probably the porter/signalman heading from the booking office, which contained the single line token instruments, to the West cabin to pass the trains in the station loop.

Plate 102 (*above*) illustrates the station buildings at Fortrose, the terminus of the Black Isle branch from Muir of Ord opened on February 1, 1894. At various locations on the system timber buildings of similar style were to be found. The photograph was taken on August 25, 1959, by which time the line was only open to goods traffic, total closure taking place less than a year later. The site is now covered by a fire station.

Plates 103 and 104 show Conon station before and after the installation in 1911 of a crossing loop. The condition of the trackwork in the earlier pictures leaves much to be desired, but in the later view dignity is restored as the staff pose at the refurbished station with new trackwork, platform, footbridge, signal cabin and signal posts.

The original stations on the Ross-shire Extension were of masonry construction and **Plate 105** is a westerly view of Edderton, during the grouping era, with the two storey station house to the right hand end. Beyond are a few sidings leading to the distillery in the background. Note the monkey puzzle tree beside the station.

Plate 106 On the same section of line, but further north, Fearn is shown on August 22, 1979, by then deprived of the usual platform accessories. It has a central two storey building flanked by low extensions on both sides, and with bay windows and a colonnade stretching between them.

Of similar form was Bonar Bridge station seen in **Plate 107** on July 18, 1931. By this time further buildings had been added beyond. The station was in fact in the village of Ardgay: Bonar Bridge itself being the other side of the Kyle of Sutherland and reached by a road bridge giving its name to the location. Recently the station has been renamed Ardgay.

The station buildings on the Sutherland Railway were generally of the typical Scottish 'but and ben' or cottage style. The example illustrated in **Plate 108** (*above*) is that at Rogart in August 1979. Along the platform is a timber building to store parcels and other small consignments.

The Sutherland Railway reached Golspie in 1868, where it erected the more commodious accommodation depicted in **Plate 109**, and photographed in May 1973. From here the railway continued only by means of the Duke of Sutherland's direct support when he undertook the construction of the line to Helmsdale. **Plate 110** shows the first station on the line, the Duke's own private station at Dunrobin, in July 1931.

On the Dingwall and Skye Railway the lesser stations had equally spartan facilities and **Plate 111** is of Achanalt in July 1961. The West signal cabin, timber station buildings and stone built staff cottage huddle together along the platform. Beyond are the permanent way tool shed and trolley garage, a loading bank and siding, and the surfacemen's bothy.

Attadale was to have been the Syke line's interim terminus on Loch Carron, until navigational considerations dictated that, despite financial difficulties, it be moved seaward to Strome Ferry. However, in 1873, three years after the opening of the line, a simple halt was provided mainly for the use of the Matheson family, friends, and servants of the surrounding Attadale Estate. **Plate 112** shows the facilities as they existed in August 1974.

A humble shelter was usually to be found on the platform opposite the main station building, such as the example in **Plate 113**. This timber waiting room at Lairg was still extant in August 1979.

Parcel sheds of similar simple style were frequently provided at intermediate stations and **Plate 114** illustrates such a corrugated iron shed, again at Lairg, in 1979. In this case a wide timber crossing across the running lines was used to back up a bus or lorry for loading after the departure of the train.

Plate 115: Goods traffic was generally dealt with in a through type timber shed, the hipped roof timber type at Bonar Bridge being a common design. Inside, a full length platform gave access, via two doors on the far side, to two or three wagons standing on the siding.

To provide accommodation for its staff throughout the system, the Highland Railway built numerous houses and cottages. **Plate 116** illustrates the Agent's cottage at Killiecrankie built in 1903. This is now in private ownership and has a quite splendid outlook to the River Garry as it flows through the Pass.

At Duirinish on the extension of the Skye line a terrace of three cottages was built adjacent to the station for railwaymen working in the neighbourhood. **Plate 117** shows these in 1974.

Signal Cabins

After locomotive and rolling stock design and livery, signal cabins probably give the clearest indication of the railway company owning the length of line along which one is travelling. The Highland Railway had a very distinctive style, but as the next few pages will prove there were in fact several variations.

Perhaps the commonest was the 'two by two' pane window design, which could be assembled to give a range of lengths and indeed several widths. **Plate 118** (*above*) is of Blair Atholl South cabin in August 1974, which has five windows on the front and two on the side, one of which has three by two panes. Culrain in **Plate 119**, pictured in June 1949, is very similar, but of opposite hand and with only two by two windows. Note the privy to the left and ground signal to the right.

Plate 120: Larger still is Forres West with nine by three windows. At the front, the middle window is of three by two panes and fixed. The alternate windows on each side can be opened by sliding behind the remainder as may the first of the side windows. The pair of windows to the locking room are three by three panes. The staging to the left was used by the signalman to exchange the single line tablet by hand. Note the modern provision of electric lighting.

On the other hand considerably smaller is the ground frame at Invershin seen in **Plate 121** (*below left*), although the vertical boarding and window still show their Highland origin. Brora, depicted in **Plate 122** (*below right*) in August 1979, at least has a porch provided together with scalloped bargeboard mouldings.

Cabins with windows of two, or three by three panes were also common and **Plate 123** illustrates a typical small example at Rogart with two 'Black 5s' about to pass. Again the roof moulding is apparent, while one of the stairway newel posts has a carved head and is probably therefore the only original.

Otherwise similar in size to Forres West on the previous page, Dingwall south cabin in **Plate 124** demonstrates the use of the same standard components in a larger and taller cabin.

A cabin raised over the tracks was to be found at Keith East, where the Highland made an end on junction with the GNSR. To afford the signalman a clear view over the stone goods shed, his cabin was mounted on a metal structure bridging the siding, as shown in **Plate 125** photographed in May 1952. Note the long stairway approach to the rear.

Towards the end of its existence the HR adopted brick built bases to its cabins. The example seen in **Plate 126** is Ballinluig South which was constructed in 1919. The upper portion still shows the typical features, although a slate roof was provided instead of the usual corrugated iron.

Viaducts

The first of the many railway viaducts constructed to the designs of Civil Engineer, Joseph Mitchell, must have been the Nairn Viaduct shown in **Plate 127**. Built in 1857 for the I & AJR, it had four spans of 55 feet bridging the River Nairn.

To carry the main line through the narrow gorge at the Pass of Killiecrankie, a viaduct of ten 35 foot spans supported the single track. The viaduct leads directly into a 128 yard long tunnel just to the south of Killiecrankie Station. **Plate 128** illustrates its wooded surroundings and should be compared with **Plate 11**.

The extension of the line from Inverness to the north necessitated a viaduct to cross the River Ness and **Plate 129** (*below*) is a contemporary engraving of the masonry structure. It had five 73 foot main spans, with four 20 foot approach spans, and was constructed in 1862.

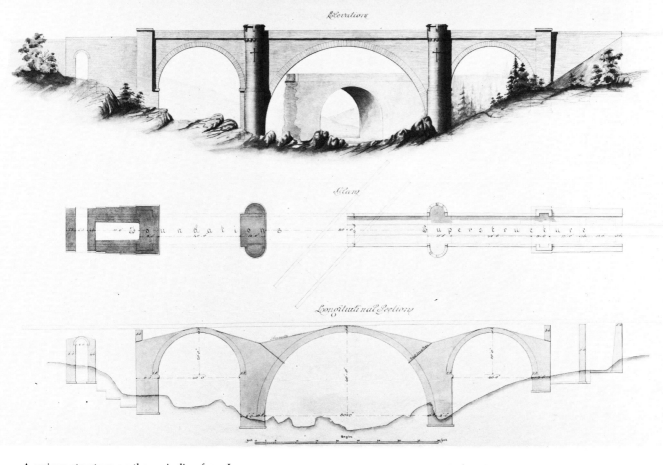

Viaduct over the River Garry

Elevation

Plan

Foundations

Superstructure

Longitudinal Section

A unique structure on the main line from Inverness to Perth was Calvine Viaduct, built in 1863 to cross the River Garry at a point where a narrow road bridge already existed near Struan station. As may be seen from the reproduction of the original drawing and the photograph – taken in July 1960 – **Plates 130 and 131**, an 80 foot semi-circular arch bounded by two 40 foot arches was used to bridge both the river and road with a single track.

The proximity of the Duke of Atholl's seat at Blair Castle resulted in the decorative turrets and pseudo arrow slits. When it became necessary to double the line at the turn of the century, the skew angles of the river, road and railway precluded the mere widening of the existing viaduct and a rather hideous lattice girder bridge was erected parallel to the masonry viaduct, part of which can be seen in **Plate 131**.

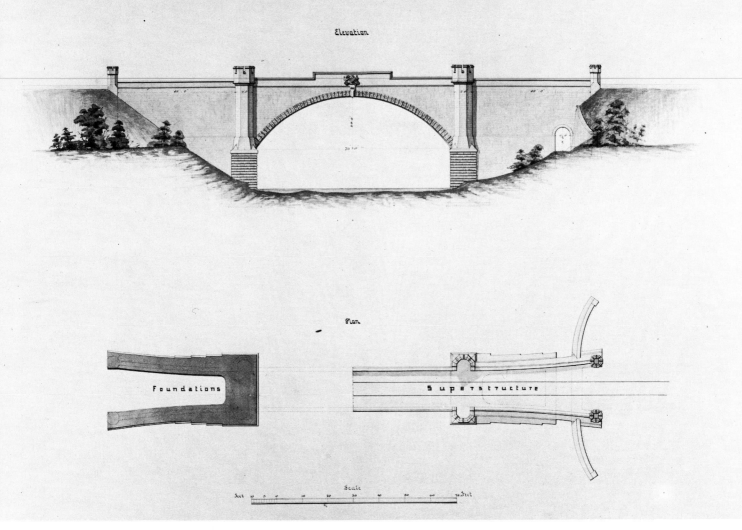

Elevation

Plan

Foundations

Superstructure

Scale

To bridge the River Braan between Dunkeld and Dalguise a 75 foot segmental masonry arch with extensive wing walls was constructed. **Plate 132** (*above*) showing the original drawing demonstrates that to please the Duke of Atholl in whose estates it lay, it too was decorated with turrets. The valley of the river is very wooded at this point and, as **Plate 133** taken in June 1967 shows, the line runs almost directly into Inver Tunnel (350 yards long).

The River Findhorn, which the Inverness to Aberdeen line crosses between Brodie and Forres, is subject to flash flooding as heavy rainfall runs off the mountains. To accommodate the river in its spate a wrought iron viaduct of three 150 foot spans formed of twin box girders and a through deck was erected in 1858. **Plate 134** (*above*) shows the extent of the structure in the 1950s and **Plate 135** the view along the track looking east in February 1923.

The Direct Line from Aviemore required several major viaducts, of which the Culloden Viaduct over the River Nairn, illustrated in **Plate 136** was completed for the full opening of the line in 1898. With a length of 600 yards it had one span of 100 foot flanked by twenty eight 50 foot spans constructed in masonry.

An example of a lattice girder steel viaduct on the Direct Line is the double track Tomatin Viaduct over the River Findhorn, depicted in **Plate 137** on June 13, 1923. This consists of nine 130 foot main spans with two masonry arches at each end.

A significant structure on the Further North line is the Oykel Viaduct over the Kyle of Sutherland built in 1868. A single 280 foot span lattice girder and five 30 foot masonry arch side spans support a single track. From the opening of Culrain Platform in 1871, the short trip of 772 yards from Invershin, for the third class fare of half a penny saved a long detour via Bonar Bridge.

The original viaduct at Beauly on the Inverness and Ross-shire Railway had been of timber construction. In 1909 this was renewed with large lattice truss main spans and plate girder side spans fabricated by Finlay of Motherwell. **Plate 139** (*top*) shows a small steam crane, equipped with a grab poised above the casing to a foundation caisson, which it is in the process of excavating on June 16, 1909. Alongside the existing timber viaduct, the replacement steel trusses and decking are being erected on a travelling cribbage as illustrated in **Plate 140** (*centre*). Subsequently the timber structure was dismantled and the new deck rolled into its place. **Plate 141** (*below*) shows 4-4-0 No. 80 *Stafford* of the 'Clyde Bogie' class built in 1886 crossing a span of the new viaduct with a goods train. Beneath the girders the original trestles are still in place and a pile of deck timbers remain to cleared away.

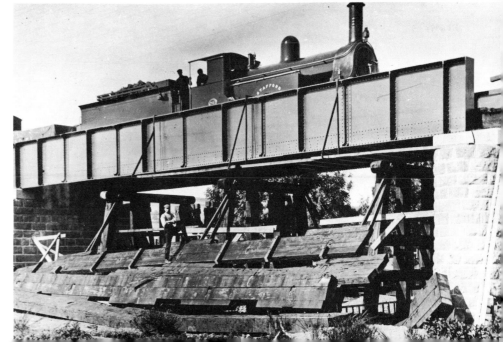

Just south of Blair Atholl the railway crosses the River Tilt in a single 150 foot span of wrought iron lattice through girders and cross girders with stone abutments. From **Plate 142** (*above*) it can be seen that the top flanges of the main girders were tied together at mid span only, while in **Plate 144**, taken in June 1967, additional bracing is in the process of being added.

Towards the end of and following World War I the need was felt amongst British railway engineers for a better understanding of the dynamic effect of locomotives on underline bridges. In March 1923 the Committee of the Privy Council for Scientific and Industrial Research set up the Bridge Stress Committee, which over the next six years conducted numerous experiments and bridge tests, resulting in its report published in 1929.

Although no Highland bridge was included amongst those tested, in view of the banishment of F. G. Smith's 'River' class 4-6-0s in 1915, on the grounds of excessive weight, the LMS clearly had an interest in the behaviour of these bridges during the passage of large express locomotives. **Plates 142, 143, 145 and 146** show tests on the previously mentioned Tilt Bridge and Tay Viaduct between Dalguise and Ballinluig on March 20, 1927. By straining a steel wire from the ground or bed of the river, readings of elastic deflection were recorded by pens on paper, some of which were mounted on revolving drums, while the locomotives crossed the bridge.

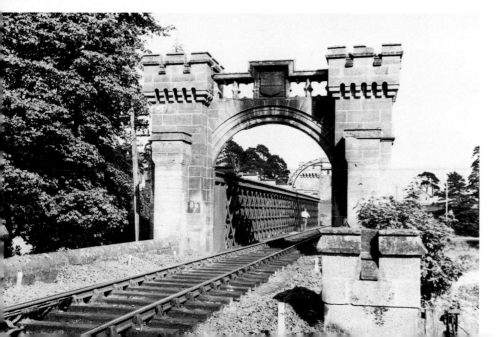

Plate 145 (*above*) shows no less than three large 4-6-0s – two 'Rivers' Nos. 14760 and 14761 together with Caley 3 cylinder '956' class No. 14803 – preparing to cross the Tay Viaduct. **Plate 146** illustrates the staging beneath upon which the deflection recorders are mounted, and the large springs necessary to tension the wires. The result was that the following year the 'Rivers' returned to work beneath Perth and Inverness.

Bridges

In 1906 Joseph Mitchell's 230 foot span, wrought iron, box girder bridge built in 1856 across the River Spey between Orton and Mulben required renewal. **Plate 147** (*below*) shows the steelwork to the new trusses in the process of being erected between the old girders. Note the temporary travelling gantry running on the top flanges of the girders and the timber falsework in the river bed.

The crossing of the River Dulnain between Broomhill and Grantown-on-Spey on the original main line was by means of an 80 foot span lattice girder through bridge. **Plate 148** is a photograph of the bridge taken in June 1967, some twenty months after the closure of the route.

Shortly after leaving Inverness the line to the north crosses the Caledonian Canal at Clachnaharry and this necessitated a swing bridge, with a total length of 126 feet. The span nearest the camera can be swung clear of the waterway by rotating the bridge about a pivot on the far bank. Beyond is the counter-balance section of the bridge. In **Plate 149** it can be seen that the ironwork has been painted white. The purpose of this is to reflect the heat of the sun, thereby reducing the expansion and contraction of the deck, which otherwise increases the size of the rail joint at each end. The mechanism was interlocked with the electric tablet between Ness Viaduct and Clachnaharry signal cabins.

Plate 150 shows Paopachy accommodation bridge on March 19, 1913, during the work of widening of the line between Clachnaharry and Lentran. The cast iron girders over the single track were replaced by a steel 'N' truss spanning two tracks. The new abutment is under construction on the right hand side.

An example of a small masonry arch is seen in **Plate 151** of a road underbridge just north of Pitlochry station.

The small stone arch depicted in **Plate 152** is to afford passage for sheep from one side of the line to the other. This example is adjacent to the Quoich Bridge near Dalwhinnie.

Many of Joseph Mitchell's masonry overbridges over single tracks were of the almost semi-circular arch form. Illustrated in **Plate 153** is Bridge No. 86H which provides access to the golf course south of Blair Atholl.

Plate 154: An elliptical shaped arch is more appropriate to a double track crossing, as this view of Bridge No. 97 at Tain demonstrates. This photograph was taken towards the end of 1922. In the background a 'Small Ben' is on shed.

Plate 155 shows a new lattice girder footbridge of standard HR design for Fearn being fabricated at the Works of Baird & Sons of Anniesland, Glasgow on June 30, 1910.

Another example of a Highland footbridge, is this view of Pitlochry station footbridge (**Plate 156**).

Permanent way

Permanent way may be less glamorous than some other items of railway equipment, but is absolutely fundamental to the railway scene. Up until grouping individual companies tended to have their own design of rail chair and the Highland was no exception, using several varieties over the decades. **Plate 157** is of a four bolt type with large fillets between the bolts dating from 1913, and found along with other types in a siding at Lairg in August 1979.

The Highland set up its main permanent way depot behind the station at Forres. Here, amongst other things, the Engineer installed a pressure creosoting plant for treating sleepers. **Plate 158** is a view looking into the cylinder filled with a train of four small narrow gauge trucks loaded with sleepers; whilst **Plate 159** (below) is of the loading bank stacked with logs and sleepers to be treated. Both photographs were taken in December 1916.

In earlier days long length timbers were not considered necessary for turnouts, as is always the case now. Instead interlaced sleeper leads were adopted. **Plate 160** (above) is of the crossing area of a survivor discovered at Ballinluig, again in 1979. Note how alternate sleepers support the far and near tracks of the turnout and also the variety of chairs in use.

In sidings the simple, but effective, point lever illustrated in **Plate 161** was frequently to be found with the company initials cast on the counterweight. This one was at Kyle of Lochalsh. These were painted black with a white counterweight.

Plate 162 depicts another standard HR item of permanent way equipment, the rail built buffer stop; this one being at Kingussie in August 1974 with the timber baulk somewhat past its best. Buffers were painted black with a red face to the baulk. Note the Highland four bolt chairs of another design to that in *Plate 157*.

Beside the track mileposts at not only mile, but also quarter, half and three-quarter intervals, were provided on the down-side to enable staff to describe a location precisely. **Plate 163** (above left) is the $59\frac{3}{4}$ mile post on the Skye line at Duirinish. Likewise, gradient posts were installed at each change in gradient in pairs, one on each side of the line. The example in **Plate 164** (*above right*) is again at Duirinish. Both mile posts and gradient posts were painted white with numerals in a chocolate colour.

Lineside

The gangs of men stationed at regular intervals along the line to maintain the track, drainage and fences needed shelter and stores for their tools. This resulted in the provision of huts throughout the length of the system, such as the one in **Plate 165** at Attadale constructed of old sleepers with a corrugated iron sheet roof.

At points where footpaths crossed the line, foot-bridges were seldom justified and to keep the lineside fence stock proof, stiles were to be found, such as the one illustrated in **Plate 166** in Drumochter Pass. These were painted a chocolate brown colour. Note that for wheeled vehicles and the supervised crossing of livestock a gate was also provided alongside.

Occupation crossing gates were also necessary at various locations and these might be constructed of timber or iron. **Plate 167** shows a wooden framed gate with iron rails, complete with a lamp and target. **Plate 168** on the other hand illustrates an all metal gate on the main line between Killie-crankie and Blair Atholl.

Platform lamps, lit by oil, were of standard design, but mounted in different forms. **Plate 169** is of the Up platform at Rogart on July 18, 1931 and shows a post mounted lamp with the name of the station on the glass.

Plate 170 is an example of a wall mounted bracket at Strathcarron, while **Plate 171** is a lamp on the corner of a standard footbridge at Dalwhinnie. Both photographs were taken in August 1974.

To advise passengers of the impending arrival of trains a hand bell was rung by station staff as soon as the train came in sight or five minutes before departure. **Plate 172** below illustrates one inscribed with the initials of the Inverness and Aberdeen Jcn. Rly.

Helmsdale in **Plate 174** on the other hand has the more usual raised letters affixed to a board mounted on square posts. Note the post finials.

Station name boards in Highland days had burnt sienna lettering and frames on a cream coloured ground. **Plate 173** shows an enamel board for Tomatin in $10\frac{1}{2}$ by $2\frac{1}{2}$ in letters together with the height above sea level in $1\frac{1}{2}$ by $\frac{1}{4}$ in size.

Plate 176 demonstrates a typical use and mounting of an enamel notice at a foot crossing of the line.

Trespass warning notices were originally painted on timber boards with a light chocolate legend on a white ground. From the 1880's a similar colour scheme was adopted in the form of an enamel notice, as in **Plate 175**. From the second decade of this century a 25 by 16 in cast iron notice was used, usually with the raised letters picked out in white on a black ground.

Platform equipment included barrows. For the larger types these were usually of the Hurley variety illustrated in **Plate 177** at Aviemore, and still in the LMS livery of grey with white lettering in 1974.

A bench seat with cast iron ends is depicted in **Plate 178** (*below*) at Keith (GNS) in 1983. The arm rest of the further end has unfortunately been broken.

A relic from Redcastle on the Black Isle branch, preserved in the Strathspey Railway's Museum at Boat of Garten, is the watering can shown in **Plate 179** (*below*)

To assist passengers board and disembark from trains at the numerous stations with low platforms, step boxes were provided. Despite the name painted upon the one in **Plate 180** (*below right*), it was photographed at Lairg, also in 1979.

Lineside features that give a strong individual flavour to a railway have already been mentioned in connection with signal cabins. The signal equipment itself equally distinguishes the owning company. On the Highland much of this was standard apparatus supplied by McKenzie and Holland of Worcester together with Dutton also of Worcester. Typical examples of the wooden post signals with tall spiked finials are shown in **Plates 181 and 182**.

Signalling

The first at Boat of Garten has a wooden starting arm over a metal skeleton shunting arm, from which a letter 'S' has disappeared, while the disc signal at the base of the post is a later addition. In the second 'Big Goods' No. 17918 approaches the Down Home signal at Slochd Crossing with the Aviemore to Inverness goods train on September 16, 1929. At a Highland single line crossing loop the second arm below a home was not a distant for the next signal, but was known as a 'repeater' and was only pulled off to indicate to the driver that the automatic token exchange apparatus was to be used.

Plate 183 depicts the Down Home signal with repeater and bracket mounted skeleton shunt signal at Dingwall. In both **Plates 182** *(above right)* **and 183** *(right)* the lamps to the home and repeater signals have been lowered to ground level by means of a chain which passed over the pulley wheel at the top of the post to a windlass mounted at the base of the post. This enabled the lamps to be attended to daily without the need to climb the post. Nevertheless, ladders were also provided to afford proper access for maintenance purposes.

Whereas normal slotting of distant arms requires three balance weights, because the long length of passing loops on the Highland necessitated a signal cabin at each end in most instances, a fourth balance weight was frequently introduced to permit the second cabin to control the lowering of the home arm *(see Figure 2)*.

Plate 184 Probably the only signal gantry on the Highland system was directly beside the Welsh's Bridge cabin on the approach to Inverness station. The famous engine roundhouse is on the left, followed by the entrance to the goods yard, the station, Lochgorm locomotive works, the Rose Street curve for through running to the North, and Needlefield carriage and wagon works with the signal cabin on the right.

Not all signal equipment on the line was of the McKenzie and Holland style. **Plate 185** depicts a non-standard installation at Wick with cruciform finials, square cornered spectacles and tapered arms. The wagons on the left would appear to be loaded with contractor's equipment used during the construction of the Lybster branch in 1902/3.

Plate 186 shows a McKenzie and Holland ground signal at Evanton, equipped with hoop bars to protect it during rope shunting operations.

Some disc shunting signals were mounted on tall cast iron pillars to afford good sighting. The enlarged base plate, to give improved stability, should be noted in **Plate 187** of an example at Rose Street, Inverness.

Plate 188 is a close up of the lamp house and red disc with a red lens mounted at the centre. Normally this was presented in the direction of the track. Pulling off the signal caused the whole lamp house to revolve 90° about a vertical axis and thereby present a white light for clear.

Plate 189 shows a level crossing for a minor road within the station limits at Rogart. Level crossings, as opposed to occupation crossings, were usually interlocked with the protecting signals. The single gates at this crossing span the two tracks of the passing loop and have therefore been stayed from the tall gate posts.

Of the 485 route miles belonging to the Highland Railway at the Grouping, together with 21 miles worked by the Company, only 47 miles was double track. The remainder was of course single line and from the 1890s most was protected by electric tablet instruments installed at the many crossing points. In an effort to reduce the likelihood of enginemen continuing into the next single line section with the token for the previous section, many lengths were rearranged by the LMS with alternate key and tablet instruments. **Plate 190** shows on the left a Tyer patent key token instrument, while that on the right is the same maker's No. 6 tablet instrument in the booking office at Rogart. Behind the instruments are the hoops and leather pouches used for the hand exchange of tokens at slow train speeds. On the Skye line the tablet bell and gong circuits were extended to the station masters' houses at crossing stations and the signalman's house at Fodderty Jcn.

To assist the hand exchange of tokens a small raised platform was often provided outside signal cabins, as seen in **Plate 191** at Slochd Crossing. In front of this is the automatic token exchange apparatus with the collecting forks in position, while behind is a lamp post with oil lamp. Below the lamp is mounted a cabinet in which the actual collecting forks of the exchange apparatus are kept when not in use. Note the point rodding beyond the tracks boxed in timber to prevent them seizing up in snowy weather.

Automatic Token Exchange Apparatus

The exchange of tokens by hand was supposed to take place at a speed not exceeding 10 mph. To obviate the delay that this imposed on through trains, all passing loops on single line sections of the system, except short branch lines, were equipped with Manson's automatic token exchange apparatus. In **Plate 192** (*left*) a tripod and lifting tackle are being used to position a precast concrete base for this apparatus.

Finally **Plate 194** (*below*) shows No. 90 *Grandtully* with its fork lowered, as it approaches the ground apparatus with the slider and forks advanced and the exchange of pouches about to take place. With this apparatus exchanges could be made at speeds up to 60 mph, although in these circumstances the collected pouches tended to be rather tightly wedged in the forks. In theory at least, speeds through passing loops were restricted to 40 mph, but perhaps this was not always adhered to!

Mounted on top of the cast iron pillar was a slider carrying the collecting forks and counterweight. By activating a lever beside the pillar, the forks carrying the leather pouch, which contained the aluminium tablet or key for the next section, could be advanced towards the track as the train was due. **Plate 193** (*above*) illustrates the slider in the retracted position with the pouch from the engine in the collecting forks.

The largest signal cabin on the Highland Railway was at Welsh's Bridge, Inverness, with 105 levers. In **Plate 195** the signalman on duty is standing beside the frame on May 26, 1930. Note the instruments mounted above the levers, while along the right hand wall can be seen telephones, a notice board on the chimney breast and the desk for the train register.

Plate 196 shows a close up of the McKenzie and Holland 'cam and tappet' type frame in the Rose Street cabin, Inverness.

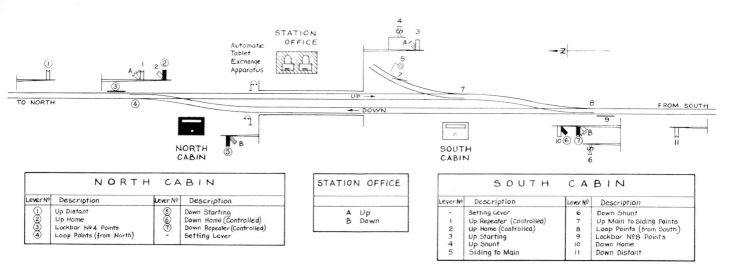

NORTH CABIN			
Lever Nº	Description	Lever Nº	Description
①	Up Distant	⑤	Down Starting
②	Up Home	⑥	Down Home (Controlled)
③	Lockbar Nº4 Points	⑦	Down Repeater (Controlled)
④	Loop Points (from North)	-	Setting Lever

STATION OFFICE	
A	Up
B	Down

SOUTH CABIN			
Lever Nº	Description	Lever Nº	Description
-	Setting Lever	6	Down Shunt
1	Up Repeater (Controlled)	7	Up Main to Siding Points
2	Up Home (Controlled)	8	Loop Points (from South)
3	Up Starting	9	Lockbar Nº8 Points
4	Up Shunt	10	Down Home
5	Siding to Main	11	Down Distant

Whilst most of the Highland's lines were single, this did not preclude the running of heavy trains. Indeed at busy times the infrequency of scheduled trains and the difficulty of fitting in additional paths, tended to enhance the need for long trains to deal with the traffic. The result was that all crossing loops were of considerable length, typically 500 to 700 yards.

At the time that absolute block working was made obligatory in 1889, the Board of Trade *Requirements and Recommendations* limited the distance from the lever to facing points for mechanical operation to a maximum distance of 180 yards. As the distance between the facing points at each end of the loops was considerably in excess of twice this figure, two lever frames were required in virtually every case. Perhaps alone amongst railways at the time, the Highland however, accorded the status of signal cabin to both. The electric tablet instruments on the other hand were generally located in the station booking office, where the station master was responsible for operating the instrument and delivering the tablet to the engine driver.

Whereas on normal double line the clearing point of a block section is usually a minimum of 440 yards in advance of the home signal, on a single line it is ordinarily at the starting signal and therefore both loops must be clear before trains can be admitted to the sections of line on both sides and hence due to cross. The Regulations require that the first train to arrive must be halted at the home signal and only allowed to enter the loop at slow speed, thus reducing the risk of over-running the starting signal. Should the second train arrive in the meantime, it is not to be admitted until the first has drawn to a stand within the loop.

Figure 2 illustrates the signalling arrangement at a typical crossing loop and shows how, by means of slotting of the signal arms, the two cabins kept mutual control over one another and also that the starting and repeater signals could only be pulled off with the sanction of the station office. The more familiar use of a slot is where a distant signal is mounted under a home arm on the same post; when unless the home is off, the slot on the distant prevents it going to the off position. As used by the Highland at crossing loops however, it is the home signal which is slotted and thus controlled by both cabins, or the starter and repeater controlled by one cabin and the station office. Thus two levers some hundreds of yards apart had to be pulled before the signal would clear.

In these circumstances, with three different locations from which trains are controlled, the staff requirement for an often small and isolated community could have been heavy. However, from the 1890s

onwards the Company introduced a number of devices to facilitate the crossing manoeuvre. An early example was the installation of 'admitting' and 'setting' levers. The admitting lever released the slot on the home signal at the other end of the loop from the cabin where the lever was situated, but locked that cabin's home signal normal, i.e. at danger. When trains from opposite directions were due to be crossed, two men went one to each cabin and each set the loop points normal and pulled the admitting lever. The signalman in the cabin at the end where the first train arrived would then restore the admitting lever which enabled him to lock his points and pull the home signal, thus permitting the first train to enter the loop with minimum delay. Once safely in the loop and at a stand and the home restored to normal, he may pull the small setting lever, set the road for the departure of the second train and pull the admitting lever again. The action of pulling the setting lever operated an indicator in the other cabin, thus advising the signalman there that he might let the second train into the loop and afterwards set the road for the departure of the first train.

Quite clearly the setting lever could be abused and the *Appendix to the Working Timetable* warns against this. Another unorthodox procedure forbidden in the *Appendix* is pulling of the distant lever before lowering the home and starting signals. This was possible in some installations, since pulling home lever released the frame locking on the corresponding distant. Due to the slots, it did not follow that the home signal would come off and the starter was in any case operated from the other cabin.

In this way the whole procedure could be carried out by just two men, the Station Master and one porter/signalman; or nowadays on the few lines still worked by this system, just one man, when a bicycle is a handy means of reducing the legwork between cabins and the office.

Following the accident at Abermule on the Cambrian Railways in 1921, the Railway Inspecting Officer commented that a signalman in charge of the instruments was to be preferred. On the Highland main line the instruments were already in the process of being moved from the station office to one of the cabins and a full time signalman then employed. This however was never carried out on the lines to the east and north, or branches. At some of the main line crossing points, resignalled in late Highland days, the second cabin was relegated to the status of a ground frame with levers for only the adjacent starter, loop points and lock bar. The main cabin had levers for all signals and, by means of Up and Down midway release bolts, could control the ground frame for either Up or Down movements only.

Operating

Having described the technicalities of the signalling arrangements at passing loops, the actual movement of trains will be examined by means of **Figure 3**.

The first train to arrive is the South bound (Up) train, which gives one long whistle as it draws to a stand at the Up home signal. The signalman may then lower that signal and allow the train to draw forward into the Up loop and stop at the Up starting signal. Its tablet is taken to the booking office and inserted in the instrument for the section to the North.

The second train must be held at the Down home until the Up train is stationary in its loop. Should the first train arrive in good time and the Down train not be booked to stop at the station, the Down line may be set through out and the automatic tablet exchange apparatus employed. To signify to the driver of this train that the apparatus will be needed, the repeater (inner distant) signal will be pulled off.

Once the tablet from the Down train has been placed in the instrument for the section to the South, the road for the Up train may be set and this train allowed to proceed on its way.

The need arises from time to time for slower trains, such as goods trains, to be overtaken by faster trains travelling in the same direction and possibly crossed with another heading the opposite way. All this can be achieved at a simple crossing loop, in the following manner. After the Up train is safely in the Up loop, the train to be overtaken, say a Down goods, draws forward into the section to the North: but, instead of continuing through to the next block post, it awaits the arrival of say a Down passenger train. Because in this instance the line is not clear to the Down starting signal, under special provisions in the regulations and only at locations listed in the appendices to

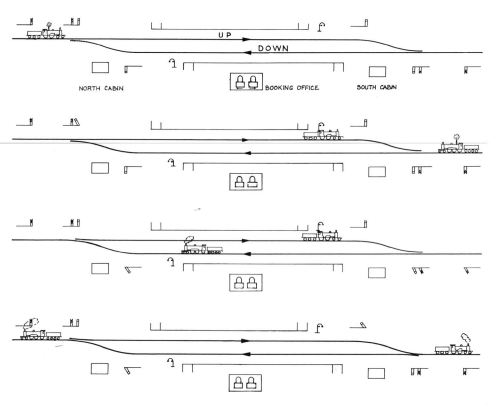

the working timetable, this train will only have been admitted into the section by the signalman at the previous cabin under 'caution'. Once the Down passenger train is in the Down loop, recently vacated by the goods, the Up train may be despatched on its way to the South. The Down goods now sets back into the Up loop, hence clearing the line to the North for the departure of the Down passenger train. The Down goods follows once the passenger has cleared the block section.

It does not require much imagination to appreciate the disruption to the timetable, particularly the planned crossing of trains, caused by any small delays and the knock on effect of these throughout the system. As we shall see, there were plenty of excuses for these delays for such diverse reasons as the late running of the overnight trains from the South (especially at peak times of traffic in mid August) to extreme weather conditions or the demands of war. All these tend to make operation of trains in these remote parts interesting to say the least.

When trains were duplicated or specials run over and above those envisaged in the working timetable, the engine of the preceeding train would carry an 'ENGINE FOLLOWING' board on a lamp iron over the left hand buffer to advise signalmen and others along the line of the additional train. **Plate 197** illustrates one of these boards, which measured 21 by 15½ in and were painted red with white lettering shaded black.

The views on this page show three eras of motive power at unidentified locations on the Perth – Inverness line during the last twenty years of the Highland's existence. **Plate 198** is of a pair of David Jones' 4–4–0 'Loch' class locomotives of 1896, with No. 129 *Loch Maree* at the head. The leading vehicles appear to be a Midland design of four wheeled ventilated van and a WCJS 45 foot clerestory family saloon. The remainder of the train is largely made up of HR vehicles of both six wheeled and bogie non-corridor coaches.

At the same site and probably on the same occassion, the next generation of motive power is seen in **Plate 199** in the form of Peter Drummond's 4–6–0 No. 146 *Skibo Castle* supplied in 1902. This and the second engine in the preceeding view both have their tablet exchange apparatus arms lowered for use, suggesting that the location is a crossing loop between stations. The train, again apparently of non-corridor stock, is a mixture of Highland and North British vehicles, some of which are six wheelers.

Plate 200: Post World War I, one of the new 4–6–0s No. 55 *Clan MacKinnon*, built in 1921, makes a fine exhaust as it climbs hard along a single line stretch with a train of vehicles of mixed origin. The first and third coaches are HR Drummond bogie lavatory stock, with a WCJS 50 foot long and 8ft 6in wide corridor composite between, followed by a clerestory passenger brake van. Note the unofficial adornment of thistle leaves and star burnished on the smokebox door of the locomotive.

Plate 201 (*above*): At the turn of the century No. 120 *Loch Ness* heads up the Caledonian main line through Luncarty with a train of 11 or 12 Highland coaches for Perth. All vehicles, except possibily one, are six wheelers and only the second is a Drummond design. The rest are from the Jones stable complete with a cord string running above the windows of all carriages to operate the alarm bell mounted on the side of the tender.

Perhaps 20 or 25 years later in **Plate 202** 'Big Goods' No. 106, fitted with brackets on the smokebox to receive the large snow plough, crosses from the Highland line at Stanley Jcn. with a mixed train for Perth. Behind the two coaches is a sheeted open fish truck, two meat vans and many more fish trucks. The rear is brought up by a passenger brake van under the overbridge.

Plate 203: Of similar vintage is an express train double headed by 'Small Ben' No. 47 *Ben a'Bhuird* and a 4–6–0 of the 'Clan' class (delivered in 1919). The train is a mixture of corridor coaches made up initially of two Caley examples, the first of 12 wheel Grampian stock, whilst the third is a Pullman dining car only introduced on the Highland in 1922.

The first line to be opened from Inverness in 1855 ran in an easterly direction and subsequently the lines from the south entered by the same route, first from Forres in 1863 and later by the Direct Line which from 1898 joined at Millburn Junction. The lines to the north however, used platforms with buffer stops adjacent to those to the east, but with the line itself curving round sharply to the north, as shown in **Plate 204** taken from the footbridge leading to the Lochgorm Locomotive Works. The Works occupied the triangle between the two lines bounded on the third side by the connecting Rose Street curve.

Upon arrival at Inverness the overnight trains from London were worked round this curve, and propelled back into the northern side of the station. The scene depicted in **Plate 204** shows the corridor train from the south early this century on the left and includes Midland and ECJS vehicles, whilst on the right a Highland train of compartment stock for the Kyle of Lochalsh waits for passengers to entrain. In the middle distance can be seen the station ground frame with a GNS train of coaches at a platform in the other half of the station.

Plate 205: At the most northerly station in the British Isles No. 130 *Loch Fannich* waits at Thurso to depart on August 29, 1923 with a train of Jones six wheel coaches for the south. the locomotive is in plain green livery and has had its louvred chimney replaced by one of Drummond style, while the number plate on the cabside is also of recent design.

Branch lines were served by tank and old tender engines relegated to secondary duties. **Plate 206** (*above*) depicts 'Skye Bogie' LMS No. 14277 in the bay platform at Muir of Ord with the train for the Black Isle branch to Fortrose on May 21, 1928. 'Large Ben' No. 14420 *Ben a'Chait* pilots 'Small Ben' No. 14404 *Ben Clebrig* with the connecting train from Inverness to the north.

The Highland's foothold in Inverness was from time to time challenged by the GNS from the east and others from the west. One grand design for a railway up the Great Glen reached partial fruition in 1903 in the form of the Invergarry and Fort Augustus Railway. This was a branch line from Spean Bridge on the West Highland's line from Glasgow which had opened to Fort William in 1894 and was extended to Mallaig in 1901. Although isolated from the rest of the system the Highland worked this rather unremunerative branch to Fort Augustus for the first four years and **Plate 207** shows 'Yankee Tank' No. 52 at Spean Bridge.

One of the few early LMS locomotive designs to find work on the Highland were the 3F Fowler 0–6–0 Ts. No. 16415, built in 1926, is seen in **Plate 208** at Hopeman with the branch train on May 16, 1928. Hopeman is a little fishing village on the north coast of Morayshire and was reached in 1892 by an extension of the Burghead branch. In addition to conveying landed fish, the Hopeman branch served a quarry at the one intermediate station at Cummingstown.

The Highland operated approximately the same number of regular goods trains as passenger, many running at night. To these must be added special trains particularly for the conveyance of fish and livestock. Just as goods engines were often used on passenger trains, so large wheeled engines normally associated with passenger trains were employed to haul more mundane trains. It was all part of the Highland's flexible use of its limited resources.

To illustrate the point **Plate 209** (*above*) is of No. 143 *Gordon Castle* hauling a train made up of railway and privately owned coal wagons, with some timber wagons and sheeted loads in the middle and a few vans at the rear. The leading wagon is a four plank mineral owned by Hunter of Murthly. The train is heading towards Perth on the Caley main line sometime after World War I.

A common duty for engines in their last days was the working of ballast trains for the Engineer's Dept. **Plate 210** shows an old Allan 2–4–0 of 1864, No. 37A, on August 31, 1923 on such a roster at Millburn, Inverness.

By the end of World War II most of the Highland motive power had been replaced by the LMS and **Plate 211** shows a double headed through freight train hauled by an ex CR Pickersgill 4–4–0 and an LMS 'Black 5' 4–6–0.

The collection of goods; loading, shunting and unloading of wagons, and final delivery of goods took up much of the railway's time and resources and some of these operations are illustrated.

Firstly, **Plate 212** is a scene at Inverness Harbour in 1918 as the Duke of Sutherland's former private locomotive 0–4–2T HR No. 118 shunts wagons on the quayside. Note the tight curves in the track, which demanded the use of locomotives with a short fixed wheelbase. The importance of such a location in time of war is emphasised by the presence of a sentry on guard outside his box behind the lighting pole.

As already mentioned the movement of livestock represented a significant, even if largely seasonal, aspect of the Highland's business. **Plate 213** depicts the cattle dock at Inverness shortly before World War II. Both cattle and sheep, together with railway staff, drovers, shepherds and collie dogs are in evidence.

Prior to Grouping the Highland relied on Wordie & Co, private carters, to collect and deliver goods at some two dozen main stations on the line. Similarly, a Mr MacAndrew operated from Golspie. Elsewhere consignees or recipients had to make their own arrangements. As can be seen from one of the carts in **Plate 214**, taken at Wick in 1939, the LMS started to take over responsibility for carting at main centres.

Special demands are placed on any railway called upon to convey royalty and the Highland was no stranger to this duty. The elaborate scene depicted in **Plate 215** is of Elgin on the occasion of the visit of Her Majesty Queen Victoria on September 6, 1872. The two evergreen triumphal arches and numerous flags are typical of the period, as are the local dignitaries along the station platform with a grandstand view and the 'hoi polloi' crowded into the overbridge in the background. Despite all the preparations the presence of umbrellas suggests that the Scottish weather is living up to its reputation.

Such an early view is nonetheless interesting for revealing items of railway detail. On the left the double sided slotted signal with separate spectacles at lower level is clearly of an old design. The water column on the right appears to be without the jacket more usual on later types for protection from the frost. The lower level platform, with simple timber steps in one case and no ramps, should be noted, together with the weed grown track formation covering the sleepers.

Another unusual feature of the Highland Railway was the arrangement whereby the third Duke of Sutherland, as a major shareholder of the Highland and owner of one of its constituents, was permitted to operate his private locomotive on the system. **Plate 216** shows the replacement to the original locomotive, which the fourth Duke had built by Sharp Stewart of Glasgow in 1895. The saloon coupled to the locomotive is one of two owned by the Duke. Both engine and saloon are now preserved in British Columbia.

The strategic significance of the north of Scotland in times of war brought particular burdens to such a small company as the Highland Railway. The bases of the Home Fleet at Invergordon and Scapa Flow required numerous naval specials for personnel and stores, and from February 15, 1917 resulted in a daily train each way between Euston and Thurso, known to those who used it as *The Misery* for obvious reasons. **Plate 217** (*above*) shows such a train at one of the northern platforms at Inverness in 1918.

During 1918 sea mines from the USA were landed at Kyle of Lochalsh and had to be transported to Invergordon for arming, prior to laying in the North Sea barrage. **Plate 218** depicts a train load of mines on September 23, 1918 outside the commandeered Dalmore Distillery at Alness. Just visible on the left is one of the five LBSC 'Terrier' 0–6–OTs acquired by the Admiralty for use on the extensive lines around the base at Invergordon.

During World War II the much larger structure of the LMS was better able to deal with the additional demands of hostilities in these parts. **Plate 219** is from a newspaper cutting dated September 2, 1939 and shows the Highland steam breakdown crane placing an RAF launch in the Harbour at Inverness.

Hazards

Adverse weather conditions were hazards the Highland often had to cope with, snow being the most frequent problem. **Plate 220** illustrates a snow drift in a cutting in the north of Caithness being charged by an engine and snow plough.

SNOW PLOUGH AT WORK

Plate 221 is of an earlier scene at Altnabreac. Here 2–4–0 Class '18' No. 24, generally in original condition, rests on completion of its work of clearing the line, with the men who partook in the task grouped in the running plate. Note the old style of signal and ornate lining on the cabside.

An early blockage of the Perth to Inverness main line was reported to the *Illustrated London News*. Their engraving, reproduced in **Plate 222**, depicts the scene at Dalwhinnie Moor as 8 foot deep drifts of snow are tackled in January 1864.

During the winter months many engines were fitted with small snow ploughs below the buffer beam. **Plate 223** shows a 'Castle', No. 140 or 146, upon arrival at the Perth ticket platform with snow piled up in front of the smokebox door, along the running plate and in the tender. In the days before steam heating in the carriages, a journey in these conditions must have been quite an ordeal.

Sometimes, if there was an obstruction buried in the snow covering the track, the result was a derailment. Such an incident occured just north of Killiecrankie station on November 23, 1893. A goods train hauled by two Jones 4–4–0s, No. 71 *Clachnacuddin* and No. 68 *Caithness*, struck an ash tree and completely left the track, as shown in **Plate 224**.

To deal with snow that had already fallen, various sizes of snow plough were provided. **Plate 225** shows William Stroudley's design for a large plough outside the Lochgorm Works in the late 1860s. The plough was attached to the front of the engine and enveloped the buffer beam and smokebox. The side flaps, which could be folded away when not in use to clear the loading gauge, and the cover to the tender should be noted. More than one engine would be required to push such a plough and as may be seen these could be used in multiple.

Once the worst spots for drifting were known, from experience, steps could be taken to prevent drifting in the future. As wind borne snow passes over a cutting, the reduction in pressure causes it to precipitate in the cutting.

Where justified, therefore, the sophisticated and expensive solution was to construct the blower seen in **Plate 226** at Forsinard. This deflects the wind down one side of the cutting, across the track and up the other side without reducing its speed and hence preventing the snow from falling to any great degree.

The alternative and more usual method was to construct a fence some distance back from the line, and often on both sides, to cause the snow to fall there and not on the track.

In the desolate regions where these are required, the adjacent landowners were usually happy to allow the railway company to construct such fences on their land, and perhaps provide shelter for the occasional sheep. The fence illustrated in **Plate 227** is at the County March Summit between Forsinard and Altnabreac.

A different use of blowers was on the Burghead branch, where the loose sand forming the dunes along the coast was blown onto the track, thereby interfering with the running of trains. The solution illustrated in **Plate 228** (*above*) was an extensive length of blowers on one side only.

On August 2, 1888 a Caledonian four wheeled covered goods van marshalled in the overnight mixed train from Perth to Inverness derailed at Dunachton between Kingussie and Kincraig. Contrary to the Board of Trade recommendations the continuous brake was not connected throughout and the following LNWR six wheel saloon, HR six wheel tri-composite and four wheel third and Pullman sleeping car were derailed. Six passengers in the composite were injured.

Plate 229 shows that clearing the line was not helped when the Cowans, Sheldon 15 ton steam breakdown crane (delivered the previous year) overturned across the underframe to the composite. In **Plate 230** recovery is in progress, made possible by a temporary track laid along the foot of the embankment.

Probably the best known accident on the Highland occured on June 18, 1914 when, following a heavy storm in the mountains north of Carrbridge on the Direct line, the spate of water in the Baddengorm Burn became bottled up against an old road bridge. When this collapsed the on-rush of water completely swept away the rail bridge a little over half a mile downstream, just as the 10 am six coach train from Glasgow to Inverness was crossing.

Railway Disaster, Carr Bridge, 18th June 1914   "Courier" Photo.

The fourth vehicle a Jones bogie brake third, seen in **Plates 231 and 232** in the stream bed, was destroyed and five passengers lost their lives. The two vehicles precariously perched on the remains of the embankment are Drummond compartment stock, whilst on top of the embankment is a CR corridor brake composite. The traffic was restored in the remarkably short time of three weeks by the civil engineering contractor, Sir Robert McAlpine.

Shipping activities

Initially the sailings from Strome Ferry were operated by steamers owned by the Dingwall and Skye Railway Company, and two vessels were subsequently taken over by the Highland in 1877. However, by 1882 these and another vessel running between Scrabster, near Thurso, and Kirkwall had been disposed of and the services operated by others.

By virtue of the Act for the extension of the Skye line to Kyle of Lochalsh the Highland acquired the right to operate the ferry services to Kyleakin and leased these operations to various parties. **Plate 233** (*above*) shows the motor launch *Sapper*, beached on March 16, 1923, with the station master Mr Reach and permanent way inspector from Dingwall, Donald McLennan, sitting on the gunwale.

In **Plate 234** (*above*), on March 16, 1923, an unnamed motor launch is seen in the water, with a steamer alongside Kyle pierhead in the background. Ferry facilities across to Kyleakin remained primitive until 1928, when the first car ferry fitted with a turntable was introduced. **Plate 235** (*left*) shows such a vessel and a motor launch with the slipway and Station Hotel behind. The car on the ferry is believed to be a Darracq 12 or 15 of circa 1925.

Hotels

At the time of the Grouping of the railways in 1923 the Highland was the proud owner of four hotels, these being at Inverness, Kyle of Lochalsh, Strathpeffer and Dornoch. It also had a third share in the hotel at Perth. **Plate 236** shows the *Station Hotel* at Inverness at about the turn of the century. On the left is the entrance to the station concourse, whilst the main door to the hotel is an extension to the original buildings on the right and was built on the site of the former south wing of the station facade. Early in World War I two enemy spies were apprehended in this hotel.

The *Station Hotel* at Kyle of Lochalsh, as illustrated in **Plate 237**, circa 1930, was in a rather more primitive architectural style. It was only in 1934 when under LMS management that it was rebuilt in the grand manner that one can still see today as the *Lochalsh Hotel*. It was partly requisitioned in 1939 by the War Department. The ferry slip can again be seen to the right of the hotel premises.

The *Station Hotel* adjoining Perth General station belonged jointly to the Caledonian, North British and Highland Railways. These were the same partners as the Perth Joint Committee that owned the station and environs. A separate parliamentary act was obtained in 1885 for powers to erect the hotel. **Plate 238** depicts the hotel, still in business in 1983.

In 1904, within a couple of years of the construction of the Dornoch branch, the Highland opened the *Station Hotel* in the town. **Plate 240** is a reproduction of an advertisement for the hotel in the public time-table for October 1915. The hotel was requisitioned in 1939.

Although traffic commenced on the Strathpeffer branch in 1885, it was not until June 1911 that the railway was ready to mark the opening of its *Highland Hotel* in the Spa by arranging a press tour. As the LMS brochure depicted in **Plate 241** shows, it was an establishment of some size and magnificence, nonetheless it too was requisitioned in 1939. Before World War I, once a week, through coaches from the south were run in a special train from Aviemore to Strathpeffer in an effort to improve patronage of the Spa. To encourage day trips on the Skye line the *Apendices to the Working Time Table* required that 'From 1st June to 30th September, Stationmaster, Kyle of Lochalsh, to wire Strathpeffer at 8.00 a.m. each morning the state of weather on West Coast, and Stationmaster, Strathpeffer, to have same posted at the Pump Room'.

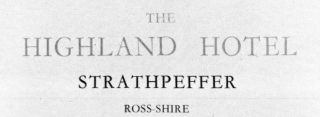

THE HIGHLAND RAILWAY COMPANY'S

STATION HOTEL,
DORNOCH

Open from June 1st to October in each year

This Large and Handsome NEW HOTEL is owned and managed by the Highland Railway Company. It stands on the finest site in Dornoch, and commands magnificent views in every direction; it faces the sea, and is beside the first Green of the Golf Course.

THE TARIFF IS MODERATE.

Inclusive Terms for Visitors staying not less than Seven complete Days.

		1st Floor Per Day.	2nd Floor Per Day.	3rd Floor Per Day.
BEDROOM BATH IN BATHROOM BREAKFAST LUNCHEON AFTERNOON TEA DINNER	... ...	15/-	14/-	12/6

All Meals served at Table d' Hôte. Fires and Baths in Bedrooms Extra.

Special inclusive Terms as above for month of JUNE, and for First Fortnight in JULY

10s DAILY

Bicycles Stored and Cleaned ... ... 0s 6d per day.
Motor Cars Stored at Owners' risk of damage by Fire or
    otherwise ... ... 2s 0d „

Postal, Telegraph, and Railway Address: "STATION HOTEL, DORNOCH."

The Highland Company's Laundry at Inverness has been enlarged in order to deal with all washing from Dornoch. Visitors' washing conveyed to and from Inverness free of charge

For further information, and for engaging Rooms, apply

THE MANAGERESS, STATION HOTEL, DORNOCH, or
H. H. WARD, HOTELS MANAGER, INVERNESS.

Publicity

To advertise the benefits of holidays and various forms of recreation possible in the Highlands, the company bedecked a car with numerous slogans and toured England, inviting passers-by to enquire and no doubt be given a leaflet or brochure, such as that in **Plate 244**. **Plate 242** shows a two cylinder 16 hp Albion motor car first used for such a purpose in 1908.

Many railway companies produced considerable ranges of postcards publicising their railway, some including views of various railway scenes and equipment. The Highland though, as **Plate 243** demonstrates, restricted itself to scenic views of the magnificent countryside to be found in the areas it served.

MIDDLE FALLS OF BRUAR STRUAN STATION

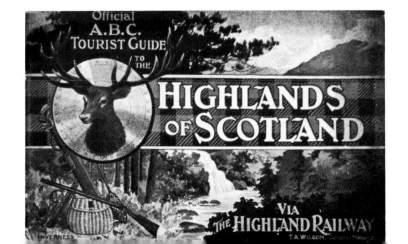

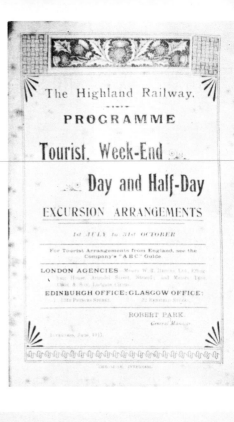

Publicity is always required to advertise additional trains, and cheap fares on special occasions, and examples are illustrated on this page. Clearly, as the poster reproduced in **Plate 245** (*above*) shows, in 1882 the Lairg holiday was expected to generate significant additional traffic if an attractive fare was offered.

For the anticipated tourist traffic from the South, a booklet was produced and distributed. The copy in **Plate 246** (*above right*) is dated June 1911.

Similar arrangements were still in operation under LMS and early BR management and **Plate 247** depicts a poster advertising cheap fares for a cattle show at Granton-on-Spey in 1935.

Railway Staff

The travelling public's and traders' opinions of a railway are considerably influenced by their dealings with ordinary members of the company's staff. Here we see a small selection of these individuals, upon whose diligence in their daily duties and their responsibilities, depended the reputation of the Highland Railway and its successors.

Employment on the railway was often a family calling and in **Plates 248** (*above*) **and 249** (*above right*) are father and son John Campbell, respectively guard on the line and station master at Lairg.

Plate 250, similarly, shows the station staff at Carrbridge in LMS uniform sometime following World War II.

Plate 251 (*left*) shows the entire staff, including probably the platelayers, lined up on the platform at Lochluichart on the Skye line.

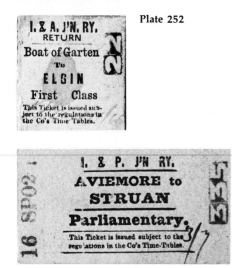

Tickets

Plate 252 (*above*) illustrates the tickets of two constituent companies. From the outset the standard colours of white for first class and green for third class seem to have been used.

The Highland Railway's ordinary tickets, shown in **Plate 253** (*right*), went through the usual stages of development. The last two have the issuing station's code number included on the ticket. The *Not available by MAIL TRAIN* on (b); and the triple entry of the departure station and destination on a single ticket on (d) should be noted.

Special tickets were required for the various forms of cheap fare and **Plate 255** (*below*) depicts examples of excursion, fishworkers and His Majesty's Forces tickets.

Plate 254 (*above*) Tickets were also issued for other facilities provided by the railway; such as sleeping car berths, steamer passage, and transport of a bicycle, or a dog accompanied by a passenger.

Plate 256 (*below*) is of two tickets from the Invergarry and Fort Augustus Railway worked for a time by the Highland.

THE HIGHLAND RAILWAY.
OFFICERS, SOLDIERS, POLICE, OR MARINERS' TICKET.

WHEN TRAVELLING ON DUTY ONLY.

No. **3530** _Third_ CLASS TICKET.

Per **3·30pm** Train, **18th October** 19**34**

From **FORTGEORGE** to **Dover South Rly**

Via *Dreadbal baul Lines Euston N.G. S.R*

		Miles.			£	s.	d.
Naval Men	at	per Mile,			:	:	
Officers	at	per ,,			*wnt.*		
Soldiers (29)	at	per ,,				:	
Do. Wives	at	per ,,			:87:	013328	
Policemen	at	per ,,				:	
Shipwrecked Mariners	at	per ,,			:	:	
Theatrical Party	at	per ,,			:	:	

_____ Booking Clerk.

☞ This Ticket to be delivered up to the Ticket Collector at end of the journey.

(A. 551)

INVERGARRY AND FORT-AUGUSTUS RAILWAY.

THROUGH SINGLE JOURNEY TICKET for Owner or Drover accompanying Live Stock by Goods Train.

No. **1**

Per _____ Train on _____ 19__

From **GAIRLOCHY** Station

To _____ Station,

On _____ Railway,

Route via _____

Not available for any other Station.

Fare paid _____

_____ Booking Clerk.

For conditions under which this Ticket is issued, see back hereof.

Parties of passengers in certain categories were catered for by the issue of special paper tickets, upon which the appropriate details might be entered. **Plate 257** (*above*) authorises the journey of 29 soldiers from Fort George to Dover, including the London Underground, on October 18, 1934.

Other forms were available for the owner or drover accompanying livestock by goods train, such as the blank I & FA version in **Plate 258** (*above right*). A form covering the free conveyance of sheep, returning from wintering in sheltered lowland areas to the more exposed uplands, is shown in **Plate 259**.

Plate 260 (*below*) All goods conveyed were accompanied by a consignment note recording the description of the goods, its weight and the charge made.

THE HIGHLAND RAILWAY.

No. **46**

_____ Station, _____ 19__

SHEEP RETURNING FROM WINTERING.
FREE PASS.

Pass _____ Sheep free of Charge from

_____ to _____

sent from this Station on _____

as per Ticket No. _____ of that date.

_____ Agent.

N.B.—This Pass must be produced and delivered to the Station Master of the Station at which the Sheep are to be loaded for the return journey, and will be his authority for entering them free of charge. The Sheep will only be returned free over the distance which they travelled by rail going to wintering; and, if returned from a Station beyond that to which they were originally booked, the Company's ordinary rates will be charged for the extra distance.

In the event of any attempt being made to substitute other Stock for that which was originally forwarded, the Company will prosecute such parties according to law

---

(A. 317) NOTICE—All Rates and Charges are to be paid on delivery of the Goods, unless the Consignee has a Ledger Account, and in that case the Account will be rendered Monthly, and must be settled within Eight Days thereafter. Errors or Overcharges, when found to exist, will be at once rectified and allowed, but while under discussion shall form no ground for delay in settling of Accounts.

Mr *Somerville*

THE HIGHLAND RAILWAY.
AVIEMORE Station, *July* 19**02**

To THE HIGHLAND RAILWAY.

McCorquodale & Co. Limited, Printers, Glasgow and London

19 02	Description of Goods	CONVEYED		WEIGHT.				Rate.	Paid on.			Cartage.			TOTAL		
		From	To	Tons.	Cwts.	Qrs.	Lbs.		£	s.	d.	s.	d.	£	s.	d.	
July 31	1 Hole 1 Bag	Dalkeith			1			10							3	0	

pro Company, *Haig* 4 4 02, Signature *Nicolson*

N.B.—For Conditions of Carriage, &c., by this Company, see back hereof.

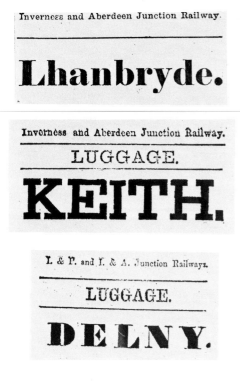

Luggage Labels

In the days when our forefathers found it necessary to be accompanied by substantial quantities of personal luggage, the railway companies provided printed labels for a large selection of destinations, and **Plate 261** (*above*) shows examples from the constituent companies. Early Highland examples for local and foreign destinations, with the heading 'The Highland Railway Company', can be seen in **Plate 264** (*below*).

In **Plate 262** (*above*) the word 'Company' is omitted from the title, but a curious mixture of serif and sans serif lettering styles have been adopted for the destinations.

The code number in the top right hand corner (A.425) indicates a later batch in **Plate 263** (*above*), two of which have had the departure station 'Blair Atholl' added by rubber stamp.

Plate 265 (*right*) illustrates the final version, with consistent printing, whilst **Plate 266** (*below*) is of an I & FAR label and post-grouping examples.

INVERNESS
(Via FORRES)

Other labels included carriage destination labels, an example of which is seen in **Plate 267**, whilst **Plate 268** (*right*) is of a mail bag label used by the Post Office.

DATE _____ TIME _____

From **London Parcel Section** **B**

To **THURSO** **B**

To be put out at **PERTH**

G.P.O.
992/FC305/37.

NUMBER OF O BAG

THE HIGHLAND RAILWAY.

EXCESS LUGGAGE—PAID

FROM

_____ Station, _____ Train,

_____ 19 _____ Packages.

A. 423) THE HIGHLAND RAILWAY.

PERISHABLE GOODS
FISH—PER GOODS TRAIN.

From KYLE OF LOCHALSH

To MANCHESTER, L. & N.-W.

Via DUNKELD, CAL., CARLISLE, and L. & N.-W.

Date, _____ 19 __ Wagon No. _____

Owner and No. on Sheet. _____

Depending on the type of fare being charged and the journey undertaken, passengers were allowed to take with them a certain amount of luggage free of charge. Luggage in excess of that laid down had to be paid for, and **Plate 269** (*above*) illustrates the label which had to be applied.

Various types of wagon label were also in use and **Plates 270 and 271** (*left*) illustrate opposite extremes. First a perishable goods – fish and secondly a return empty label, the last three lines of which are printed in vermillion.

(A. 443)

INVERGARRY AND FORT-AUGUSTUS RAILWAY.

From *Fort. Augustus*

TO HOME EMPTY.

Via *S.bge. & NB*

Date, *2. 5. 03.*

IMPORTANT.—When Foreign Wagons are returned Empty THEY MUST BE LABELLED BY EXACTLY THE SAME ROUTE (NAMING ALL JUNCTIONS) AS RECEIVED.

Spotlight On . . .

AVIEMORE

Following the opening of the Direct Line on November 1, 1898, Aviemore became an important station for the marshalling of trains to and from the new route, via Carrbridge, and the original line, via Forres with connections to the eastern points on the system. The rearrangement of passenger trains at Aviemore also often included the sorting of through coaches into portions for the west and east coast routes to England respectively. For much of the year these portions would be formed as a combined train to Perth, but in the busier summer months they would be run as separate trains. **Plate 272** shows No. 145 *Murthly Castle* having arrived with an Up train late one summer afternoon, probably in 1924. The first coach is a 65 ft 6 in ECJS 12 wheel brake composite of NER design, followed by an ECJS sleeping car. Behind the station name board on the right is a 12 wheeled Pullman buffet car, *Helen MacGregor* built in 1914 by Cravens, which will be included in the train to provide an evening catering service to passengers on their way South.

Further south Blair Atholl represented an equally important staging point, with locomotive facilities at the foot of the climb up the 'Hill' to the Pass of Drumochter. **Plate 273** illustrates one of Peter Drummond's 'Barney' class, No. 139 with a goods train, about to enter the single line section leading South.

BLAIR ATHOLL

Blair Atholl attracted the attention of several railway photographers over the years and the two views on this page are of double-headed trains about to depart from the southern end of the station in early LMS days. **Plate 274** is of No. 14413 *Ben Alligan* built by Lochgorm in 1901, leading another 4–4–0 No. 14523 *Durn* supplied by Hawthorn Leslie in 1916. No. 14413 is in the LMS crimson lake livery and was one of the few 'Small Ben' class not to be rebuilt with a Caley standard boiler. Probably as a result it was withdrawn relatively early at the end of 1933. No. 14523 too, as one of a class of only two engines, was taken out of service only 16 months later.

The two 4–6–0 engines in **Plate 275**, both also in crimson lake, on the other hand were longer lived. No. 14682 *Beaufort Castle,* built by Dübs in 1902, survived until nearly the end of 1943, whilst the second engine No. 14767 *Clan Mackinnon* was the last of its class to be withdrawn in early 1950. When photographed both these engines were equipped with Westinghouse brake, as well as the usual automatic vacuum brake gear. No. 14682 has been fitted with a rather ugly non-standard large flat topped dome cover. On the lefthand side the South signal cabin can just be seen, with the automatic tablet exchange apparatus set for the passing of a Down train.

Across the River Tilt and half a mile from Blair Atholl station an occupation bridge provides access to the local golf course. In **Plate 276** 'Castle I' class, LMS No. 14678 *Gordon Castle* in lined black livery is seen passing under this bridge, as it heads south with a train carrying lamps indicating an express; however the first two coaches at least are bogie compartment lavatory stock. This engine was withdrawn first in June 1939, but due to the shortage of engines during World War II and as it had not been cut up at the time, it was reinstated 15 months later and finally retired in February 1946. Note the unusual small knob on the left hand side of the smokebox door.

The 'Castle' class locomotives were built in three versions and **Plate 277** illustrates LMS No. 14693 *Foulis Castle,* the last of the third series supplied by the North British Locomotive Company in 1917. This series of just three engines was fitted with 6 foot diameter driving wheels, six wheeled tenders and screw operated reversing gear. No. 14693 without lamps is departing from Blair Atholl with a north bound train, whilst one of David Jones' 'Big Goods' class waits in a siding to follow on the climb to the summit.

DINGWALL

At the head of the Cromarty Firth, 18½ miles north of Inverness, Dingwall was the county town of Ross and Cromarty and an important staging point for the Skye line and later the junction for the branch line trains to Strathpeffer. **Plate 278** depicts the scene at the northern end of the station shortly before World War I. No. 7 *Ben Attow*, has arrived with a Down train and 0–4–4T 'Passenger Tank' class No. 25 *Strathpeffer* waits with the branch train in the bay platform.

Plate 279: At the other end of the station another 4–4–0 'Small Ben', No. 14398 *Ben Alder* in LMS crimson lake livery and coupled to an eight wheeled tender, stands with an Up train, probably in 1925. The first three vehicles of the train are horse boxes, including a Caledonian six wheeled double ender. Following reboilering in 1929, No. 14398 continued in revenue earning service until February 1953, when as the last of its class it was laid aside for preservation. Unfortunately this came to nought and she was sent for scrap in 1966.

INVERNESS

The headquarters and hub of the Highland system was at Inverness. **Plate 280** shows an express train for the South in the 1890s passing Welsh's Bridge signal cabin. The train is hauled by a pair of David Jones' 4–4–0s of the 'Strath' class supplied by Neilson Reid in 1892. No. 93 *Strathnairn* is leading and the train is made up of through coaches for various lines with Highland coaches at the rear.

In **Plate 282** (*below*) at almost the same spot early this century one of Peter Drummond's 'Small Ben' class No. 17 *Ben Alligan*, built at Lochgorm in 1901, sets off from Inverness. All the stock is in the two colour livery of dark olive green with white upper panels. This livery was superseded in 1907 by the all green style. The engine is already in the unlined green livery introduced in 1902. The leading coach is a Jones 46 ft 3 in bogie lavatory third supplied by Brown Marshall in 1893 and is followed by a Drummond six wheeled passenger brake van.

Further views of the eastern approaches to Inverness in LMS days show, in **Plate 283** (*above*), 'Skye Bogie' class No. 14279 drifting past the Engineer's permanent way loading bank on June 17,1927. The wide range of goods vehicles in both pre- and post-grouping liveries in the background should be noted (*see reference accompanying Plate 20*)

In **Plate 284** an unidentified 'Loch' class 4–4–0 rolls into Inverness with a through train from Aberdeen made up of LNER owned pregrouping stock.

Plate 285 taken on June 18, 1937, depicts No. 14689 *Cluny Castle* paired with a Stanier 4–6–0 5P5F, No. 5160, passing Welsh's Bridge signal cabin, as they start from Inverness with the 3.45 pm train to Aviemore via Carr Bridge. The train has through coaches to Glasgow (Buchanan Street), including one from Wick, and Edinburgh (Waverley).

KILLIECRANKIE

Symptomatic of some of the extreme difficulties of finding a route for a main line railway through the Grampian Mountains is the threading of the Pass of Killiecrankie. Leaving the broad strath from Pitlochry the single line begins to hug the side of the gorge of the River Garry, crosses Killiecrankie Viaduct and passes through one of only three tunnels on the whole of the system. Indeed at the time of writing, this stretch of the A9 highway remains one of the few unreconstructed lengths and some elaborate engineering works will be necessary.

In **Plate 286** (*above*) a 'Castle I' class 4–6–0 can be seen hauling a southbound train early this century. Whilst in **Plate 287** the photographer looks down on the viaduct as a Stanier 'Black 5' crosses with a Down express during a winter in the 1950s.

A. 425).
THE HIGHLAND RAILWAY.
LUGGAGE.
From BLAIR-ATHOLL
TO KILLIECRANKIE

Emerging from the tunnel and a short cutting, the lines curve sharply – resulting in speed restrictions in both directions of 30 mph for passenger trains and 20 mph for freight trains – and enter the passing loop at Killiecrankie station. **Plate 289** (*above*) depicts the scene on May 15, 1928 looking from the road overbridge towards the South signal cabin, the Agent's house and railway staff cottages, and with the slopes of Ben Vrackie in the distance. Note the examples of McKenzie and Holland signals with wooden posts, which were soon to be replaced. Killiecrankie was one of many stations where the use of towing ropes was authorised on a regular basis to shunt vehicles, in this case for traffic by Down trains on the Down Loop. The tow rope was kept on posts at the lineside, when not in use.

Looking in the opposite direction, from the same spot on the same day, **Plate 290** captures a reboilered 'Loch' class 4–4–0, LMS No. 14392 *Loch Navar*, ambling South with a mixed freight train. The position of the lamp incorrectly suggests it is a 'shunting engine working exclusively in station yards and sidings'! The North cabin can be seen in the distance.

THE SKYE LINE

That long limb of the Highland Railway, the Skye line, reached across from Dingwall on the East coast of Scotland. At first from 1870, the line terminated at Strome Ferry on Loch Carron, but from 1897 it was extended to Kyle of Lochalsh to give improved access to the Hebrides. Steep gradients, tight curves and a limit on the size of permitted locomotives often resulted in unusual types working on the line. **Plate 291** depicts No. 131 *Loch Shin*, the largest class permitted at the time, followed by No. 34 of the 'Skye Bogie' class specially developed for use on the line. They were photographed at Kyle on August 31, 1923.

From 1928 the LMS allowed the 4–6–0s of the 'Superheated Goods' class to work to Kyle. This resulted in most of the eight engines of this class being retained until after 1946, when the turntable at Kyle was renewed, thus permitting the Stanier 5P5Fs to displace them. **Plate 292** shows 'Superheated Goods' LMS No. 17957 passing Loch Garve with an east-bound train on September 16, 1937.

THE MOUND

On its opening in 1868, The Mound station was the nearest rail access to the Royal Burgh of Dornoch. This could be reached by the causeway for a highway constructed across the estuary of the River Fleet by the engineer Thomas Telford in 1816. In 1903, however, a light railway was completed from The Mound to Dornoch and **Plate 293** illustrates The Mound station following the rearrangements necessary to make the junction with the branch line. Through the bridge the station is seen, between the main line to the north and the branch, which falls quite steeply to the righthand side.

In **Plate 294** a 'Castle I' class 4–6–0 with a south-bound train pauses at The Mound in LMS days to transact business, while the tail end of the branch line train can be seen on the right. Note that during the intervening period the wooden bracket signal has been replaced by a lattice steel version.

ACKNOWLEDGEMENTS

A work of this nature is only made possible with the help and good-will of many people and organisations, who by readily assisting the author with his enquiries and making available suitable material have enabled him to present to the reader the wide range of illustrations and supporting text. In this instance I am particularly grateful to the following for the use of the photographs reproduced:

Duke of Atholl: 130 and 132.

A. J. Bowie: 36, 37, 41, 48, 50, 149, 220 and 221.

W. E. Boyd: 52 and 58.

British Rail: 242.

A. Brown, & Co.: 237.

H. C. Casserley: 9, 20, 27, 46, 70, 76, 79, 94, 96, 107, 109, 110, 119, 169, 195, 206, 208, 227, 283, 288 and 290.

W. D. G. Chalmers Collection: 38, 68, 147, 185, 194, 204, 232, 267, 285 and 293.

G. Cobb: 236.

J. A. G. H. Coltas: 47, 59, 61 and 78.

J. M. Craig: 49, 276 and 277.

T. David: 259, 261, 270 and 271.

A. G. Ellis collection: 12, 29, 79, 205, 223, 231, 273, 274, 280, 282 and 291.

D. Geldard collection: 252, 253, 254, 255, 256, 257, 258 and 281.

W. Grey (courtesy J. H. Price): 198 and 199.

G. Heathcote: 63.

B. Hilton: 73.

Historical Model Railway Society: 2 and 88.

J. Hooper collection: 74.

Illustrated London News (courtesy Trustees of National Library of Scotland): 129 and 222.

Imperial War Museum: 212, 217 and 218.

Knight: 14.

G. E. Langmuir: 25.

LCGB Ken Nunn collection: 182 and 210.

LGRP (courtesy L. T. George): 16, 84 and 127.

Locomotive Publishing Co. (F. Moore): 3, 23 and 55.

A. MacIntyre: 207.

A. A. MacLean: 187 and 196.

Martin: 17.

J. Munro: 286.

National Railway Museum (Crown copyright): 40, 56, 197, 272 and 279.

Philco: 98.

Photomatic: 22, 30, 62, 71, 83 and 101.

P. Ransomes-Wallis: 43, 57, 60 and 65.

Real Photographs (courtesy S. Rhodes): 213 and 214.

Royal Commission on the Ancient and Historical Monuments of Scotland: 26, 93 and 105.

H. Salmon (courtesy Stephenson Locomotive Society): 6, 7, 8, 202 and 209.

Sanderson Photo: 215.

W. A. C. Smith: 89, 90 and 102.

I. R. Steel collection: 33 and 35.

W. O. Steel (courtesy R. J. Essery): 86, 103, 104, 174 and 183.

J. L. Stevenson: 125.

G. Stilley: 126.

I. H. Stockley: 116.

Strathspey Railway Museum (Dale collection): 15, 28, 34, 39, 77, 135, 137, 139, 140, 142, 143, 145, 146, 150, 154, 155, 158, 159, 173, 192, 193, 225, 228, 233 and 234.

J. Templeton: 66, 69, 72, 75, 87, 100, 120, 123, 134 and 226.

Tuck: 24.

H. N. Twells collection: 177, 241 and 247.

Valentine: 11, 32 and 243.

I. Vaughan: 167.

D. Wheeler: 172.

W. H. Whitworth: 4.

G. L. Wilson: 10, 18, 80, 81, 121, 128, 161, 166, 175, 176, 181, 186, 191, 211, 250 and 287.

G. W. Wilson: 21.

The remaining material is either from the author's camera or comprises uncredited prints from this collection.

In addition to the aforementioned contributors, others have assisted in more general ways and my thanks are due to the staff of the Inverness Museum and Art Gallery and the National Motor Museum at Beaulieu; members of the Historical Model Railway Society, the LMS Society and the Transport Ticket Society; together with numerous railwaymen in the Highlands who have responded with friendliness to my enquiries. Finally the production of this book has only been possible with the help of Marion Stockley and Joan and Alan Batten, together with the forebearance of my wife and sons.

For members of the Strathspey Railway Company and Association the pleasure to be derived from a steam operated railway in the Highlands continues and a public service is run during summer months on the preserved line open between Aviemore and Boat of Garten. Twice a week the Boat Hotel charters a train and offers haute cuisine aboard with the magnificent vista of the Cairngorm Mountains in the evening light as a back drop.

Plate 295 depicts No. 60, a Hunslet 0–6–0ST, on May 26, 1983 marshalling the coaches for the 'The Boat Train' under the supervision of the volunteer signalman and his lady.